THESAURUS
of extremes

THESAURUS
of extremes

MICHAEL HATCH

├─── verbal extremes and everything in between ───┤

D&C

David and Charles

A DAVID & CHARLES BOOK

David & Charles is an F+W Publications Inc. company
4700 East Galbraith Road
Cincinnati, OH 45236

First published in the UK in 2008
First published in the USA in 2007 as 'Orders of Magnitude'
by Writer's Digest Books Cincinnati, Ohio

A catalogue record for this book is available from the British Library.

ISBN-13: 978-0-7153-2974-0 paperback
ISBN-10: 0-7153-2974-x paperback

Printed in Finland by WS Bookwell
for David & Charles
Brunel House   Newton Abbot   Devon

For David & Charles
Editorial Assistant: James Brooks
Art Editor: Sarah Clark
Production Controller: Roger Lane

Visit our website at www.davidandcharles.co.uk

David & Charles books are available from all good bookshops;
alternatively you can contact our Orderline on 0870 9908222 or
write to us at FREEPOST EX2 110, D&C Direct, Newton Abbot,
TQ12 4ZZ (no stamp required UK only); US customers call
800-289-0963 and Canadian customers call 800-840-5220.

DEDICATION

This book is dedicated to my parents, Steve and Dr. Trish Hatch, without whom I would not exist. Thanks for putting up with my curiosity long enough for those encyclopedias to arrive, not to mention providing a paragon childhood of health, safety, warmth, and constant support, combined with just the right amount of challenge, moral guidance and love. That launching pad remains, to this day, a source of strength and bubbling vim. I love you both very much, and I really, really, really like existing. So thanks for that too.

Acknowledgments

The following people all helped at one point or another with producing the book, or with the lists and their orderings, from being sources of research, to sitting down with me for hours and giving your thoughts. This book is better because of your contributions. You each have my gratitude, just not all at once.

(In alphabetical order, starting at L, and ending with K.)

Erin Locke; George Lucas; Suzanne Lucas; Mike Lukens; Greg Lytle; Derek Martis; Armen Mauradian; Alex "MacBain" McClain; Francis McFadden; Robert McKee; Doug Meester; Shawn Metts; Isaac, John, Kathy, Paul, Patrick, and Melody Meyers; The Microsoft Corporation; Lauren Midori Kuntz; Mike Mikulics; Mirriam; Marcus Monticelli; Greg Morgan; Lauren Mosko and F+W Publications; Christina Naify; NationalBanana.com; Lucky Nguyen; The O'Brien family of Wake Forest, NC; The Onion; "Mr. Pledge" (Chris Loya); Ayn Rand; Roget; Carl Sagan; Paul Sarkis; George Shenefelt; Phil Sexton; Laura Smith; Sarah Stanley; Nick Starfield; Jesse Stern; Jeff Suess; Thesaurus.com; Kristin Thornton (Gumdrum); Jacob Joseph True; Chrissy Tsai; Marina Vainshtein; Dave, Kevin, Pam, and Ryan Wakefield; Brandon Webster; Webster's; Eric West; Wikipedia; Jenny Wood; The World Almanac and Book of Facts; the World Book Encyclopedia; Prof. David Yerkes; Julian Zajfen Esq.; Bob, Janet, Jerry, and Katie Zucker; Zucker Productions; Alpha Delta Delta of Chi Psi; Oyinlade Ayandele; Jody Bates; Jason Benesh; Eric Bowers; Sean Burns; Colleen Camp; Joseph Campbell; Lloyd Campbell; Ed Chau; Mike Chouinard; CIA.gov and the World Factbook; Manuel Correa; Amelia Cox; Richard Dawson; Travis Dejournett; Dictionary.com; Cori Doherty; The Encyclopedia Brittannica; Steve Esquivel; John "Uncle" Farhat; Scott Francis; Eric Friedman; Jane Friedman; Kevin Geary; Sean Gesell; The Golden Bear Battalion; David Green; Erica Hamm; Dr. Bill Hartman; Allison, Brian, Courtney, Greg, Mary, Tom, Bill, Phyllis, Ralph, Steven, Trish, and Vanessa Hatch; Greg Hatfield; Peyton Healey; Gary Heidt and Stephany Evans at the Imprint Agency; Karl Iglesias; Michael and Sabine Kasper; Brendan Kenny; Misha Krepon

About the Author

Photo courtesy Jerry Zucker

Michael Hatch was born on New Year's Eve, 1980, in Riverside, CA, to Steve and Trish Hatch, making it under the wire for the tax deduction by a mere 35 minutes. He became an Eagle Scout at age 17, briefly attended UC Berkeley, and now works as an 'Untitled Creative Person' at the comedy Web site NationalBanana.com.

TABLE OF CONTENTS

INTRODUCTION

THE WONDER OF DESCRIPTION

I've been a habitual quantifier for as long as I can remember, so allow me to explain why I love it. I call it 'scale awe.'

When I was four years old, I remember looking at an astronomy book that described the size of the Earth. I was riveted. The next page comparatively illustrated the sizes of the planets. There they were, a delightfully uniform spread of empty circles labeled 'Mercury', 'Earth', 'Jupiter', and so on. But the pleasant array was interrupted by a slightly curved line streaking across the page. Odd.

The book explained that the line was a demonstration of the size of the sun – and something clicked. I almost dropped the book, agape at the raw scale. That moment held deep power, and the memory is like a feeling akin to cracking a safe – without knowing the code or damaging the safe – and then not remembering how I got it open.

FOR THE LOVE OF LISTS

The earliest legitimate proto-list I can remember conceiving was 'pop quiz, quiz, test, exam, final'. I ordered these words in my mind. Once I did, the itch was scratched and the moment forgotten, somewhere around second grade. There are dozens of such examples over the course of my life. So if I've always been doing this, why did I wait until I was 22 years old to let my lists multiply across a pad of paper and, eventually, book shops nationwide? Because I failed to write them down.

On the pulsating electronic music bar of the mind, an idea has to reach a certain volume to be worth committing to ink. The sad thing is that occasionally you have an idea that's so good, you're certain you'll remember it, so you don't write it down, and then your enthusiasm sparks distraction. While you're not looking, the thing retreats back to the thicket in pieces until, if you're lucky, years later the right stimulus draws them out from the undergrowth and recombines them into something that can revive the concept, or at least trigger the memory. Like two mighty electrodes approaching ominously, once this particular idea touched paper, it exploded in fractal permutations across the page. I came *this* close to jotting my lists down or typing them out for years, but I just never quite clicked that synaptic ratchet into place to grab a pen and scribble. So how did it finally happen?

University of California – Berkeley, Spring 2002, room 2050 of the Valley Life Sciences Building, sitting somewhere near the top row of the 400-seat lecture hall on the professor's left, was an undergraduate child who, to this day, still can't remember what that class was about.

So I'm sitting there, doodling, and I recall a thought I had the night before as I was falling asleep with a Stonehenge documentary on. 'Monolith. Cool word ...' I'm doodling, coming loose from the dock, remembering that programme, and ... 'Monolith, that's even bigger than boulder. Epicer*. Rock's smaller than boulder.' And I start writing: 'Stone bigger than rock ... Oh! Pebble! ... Megalith!! GIGAlith!!!'

Once that second metric prefix arch-stoned into position, the dam burst. It was as if I were teetering on the brink of a sneeze for twenty years and that sneeze finally hit me while conveniently alone in a meadow where no hand need cover the plume. That $1.35 legal pad became endless rolling fields of creative freedom. There I sat, experiencing a combination of feeling, thought, and arrogance only possible to those 22-year-olds foolish enough to be absolutely convinced they're going to be a household name. Knowledge came in a flash faster than the words, which eventually got around to describing it:

'I am going to be a thing.'

In that moment, I experienced something rarely gifted to the conscious mind (and to many never at all) but which I think I've found a way for you all to share. Like a Delta-Force emotion held in deep reserve in all our subconscious oceans, and only breaching through the surface as a reward when a completely new idea is willed into being, I was source and privy to an explosively flowering, connect-the-dots infinity. An experience whereafter, for a time, the world seemed to have taken on a sort of fluffy white iridescent snuggly tinge. Awareness was experienced as a state of highly pressurized, glorious angst during which I was afraid to walk, or drive, or exist for even a second outside a self-sustaining vault at the center of the Earth on the off chance I might get hit by lightning or a meteor before the revelation could be shared. Like love.

By the end of that lecture, there were 15 lists on half-a-dozen pages, averaging around a dozen words each. As I furiously scribbled, I thought, 'I am so going to have to talk about this one day when I write the introduction to my book.' And the feeling didn't end with the lecture; it was reborn in delightful variety at the beginning of each new list. It's a feeling you can join me in, and about which I'll explain more later.

THE CREATION OF THE LISTS

I begin by starting with at least two of what I call 'handrail' words. For example: 'cold, chilly, warm, hot', which define the 'slope' of the list, which becomes its vector through the nebuloid matrices of the lexicon. This sets the 'rule' of the list, or the parameters that define it. Working within those limits and finding as many words as possible, I then rank them after much research and with great attention to detail. Of course, words aren't always lead boxes in rows – language can be very fluid. Indeed, what a Neptunian would call chilly might describe a lower temperature than what a Venusian calls cold. Think of each word as a bell curve resting upon that previously mentioned vector, with a rounded peak representing the average usage. Each list, therefore, is an arrangement, not of absolute use, but of a hierarchy of averages. Usually, chilly is warmer than cold. While some lists are more open to interpretation, others are hard and fast, such as Chain of Command (one-word military rank).

In developing these lists, I found source material in everything from Indian epic poetry to obscure laboratory lingo. I sometimes pulled from known indo-European root words, prefixes, and suffixes. Other times I made a homage to a widely known piece of art or history, especially one that had an untapped oomph I could utilize (see: Jarjaric*, **). There are some words that are just pure id babble: 'You look like a Jennifer', that sort of thing. Often, I tried out all these strategies and then decided which word from those options I thought would be the most useful.

In addition to drawing from the totality of the English language, you'll discover that I have also coined my own terms and added them to the lists. I put a single asterisk (*) by each new word I devised or applied in a new way. I put a double asterisk (**) when my contribution was significantly less, when the creative work of making the word in question bear the definition that has placed it at that particular rung has mostly been accomplished by another. An explanation of each new word can be found in the glossary.

MAKE-IT-YOURSELF LIGHTNING IN A BOTTLE

As children, my brothers (Brian and Greg) and I would combine random ingredients from around our kitchen into blended experiments and wonder, 'Are we the first people to ever try this food? To taste the combination of rice cake, pickle juice, oregano, and mustard?'

'One small step for a man.'

'Mr. Watson come here.'

'High five, Tenzing!'

Being the first one to accomplish anything is lightning in a bottle, and much of the pleasure of this project is that with every list, I am the first to ever see those words in that order. Ever. When I make a new list, I get the initial exposure to the data, and the first chance to derive the rules that govern it. Then, using these rules, combined with my own outside knowledge and research, I can invent words that send the list ends screaming at impossible speeds so far in one direction that they sometimes come back around the other way. I'm wielding dibs on breaching the obsidian wall of what has not yet been imagined, and once there I can continue the line into the purple empyrean void and pave the road with the marble I think is pretty.

Beyond that wall, I've discovered a bliss and I've lingered there too long alone. Join me. Explore not just the lists on these pages, but the very idea that unites them. Make your own lists, be the first ever to set eyes upon your own personal orderings. Tinker with them and make your own new words, then let your linguistic offspring scamper across our cultural Galapagos and see if they thrive. The handiest will reproduce each time they're used by others. We're all in the race; I just got a head start, took the first lap by myself, and now wish to run alongside you and share in your relishing of the experience of original thought. That gem moment is available to us all. This is our language; let's help it grow with purpose and enjoy the process together. I look forward to your contributions.

IDEOLOGIES
& PRINCIPLES

I. THE GREAT CHAIN OF BEING
Medieval Christian Theology

1. Vacuum/nothing
2. Mineral/inanimate
3. Fire
4. Plants
5. Beasts
6. Humans
7. Angels
8. Principalities
9. Virtues/fortresses/ strongholds
10. Rulers/authorities
11. Powers
12. Dominions
13. Thrones
14. Cherubim
15. Archangels
16. Seraphim
17. God

II. ISLAMIC SHI'A RELIGIOUS AUTHORITY

1. Tribal Sheikh
2. Sheikh/da'ii
3. Hujjat
4. Allama
5. Ayatollah
6. Grand Ayatollah
7. Imam
8. Muhammad
9. Allah

III. ISLAMIC SUNNI RELIGIOUS AUTHORITY

1. Imam
2. Muhammad
3. Allah

IV. ROMAN CATHOLIC RELIGIOUS AUTHORITY

1. Altar boy
2. Eucharistic minister
3. Deacon
4. Priest
5. Monsignor
6. Bishop
7. Archbishop
8. Cardinal
9. Pope
10. Doctor of the Church
11. Jesus Christ
12. God the Father/ YHWH/I Am That I Am

V. Religion From Mainstream to Weird

*From a completely subjective, unfair, oversimplified,
sort of Middle-America-ish perspective, and definitely
<u>not</u> the author's worldview*

1. Protestantism (various)
2. Anglicanism
3. Catholicism
4. Judaism
5. Islam
6. Buddhism
7. Mormonism
8. Hinduism
9. New Age
10. Shamanism/ancestor worship/tribalism
11. Wicca
12. Zoroastrianism
13. Voodoo
14. Satanism
15. Scientology
16. Kabbalah

Angels
1.7

VI. Order of the Age at Which You First Realize the Truth About ...

1. 'I am' (your own existence)
2. Objects still existing in the absence of perception
3. How to use the bathroom
4. The Tooth Fairy
5. The Easter Bunny
6. Santa Claus
7. Where babies come from
8. How democracy works
9. Libido
10. Everything
11. The fact that there are lots of other religions out there and that, mathematically, there will always be more people that believe in all the other religions combined than believe in yours
12. Alcohol
13. Sex
14. The real world/life isn't fair/value of a pound
15. Nothing
16. True, romantic love
17. What it feels like to be a parent
18. The reality that – because no two people have identical internal systems of opinion – in democracy, politics is compromise (as it should be, and you're never going to really like either candidate so the choice will always be the lesser of two evils ... so get over it)
19. What it feels like to be a grandparent
20. What it feels like to be a great-grandparent
21. God/the afterlife/ re-incarnation (but not 'til you're dead)

VII. BAD TO GOOD

1. Lecteric**
2. Incomprehensible*
3. Mengelic*
4. Unthinkable
5. Horrifying
6. Unspeakable
7. Abominable
8. Execrable
9. Abhorrent
10. Opprobrious
11. Horrendous
12. Atrocious
13. Jarjaric**, *
14. Heinous
15. Vile
16. Horrible
17. Revolting
18. Horrid
19. Infamous
20. Reprobate
21. Atrocious
22. Wicked
23. Repugnant
24. Terrible
25. Evil
26. Repulsive
27. Beastly
28. Deplorable
29. Loathsome
30. Despicable
31. Awful
32. Foul
33. Detestable
34. Dreadful
35. Bad
36. Unacceptable
37. Lousy
38. Poor
39. Unpleasant
40. Dissatisfactory
41. Ordinary
42. Not Bad
43. Hunky-dory
44. Neat
45. Swell
46. Peachy
47. Good
48. Fine
49. Distinguished
50. Praiseworthy
51. Spiffy
52. Dandy
53. Exceptional
54. Premium
55. Remarkable
56. Capital
57. Commendable
58. Primo
59. Crack
60. Something Else
61. Great
62. Notable
63. Terrific
64. First-rate
65. Meritable
66. Bang-up
67. Smashing
68. Exemplary

69. Cat's pajamas
70. Extraordinary
71. Outstanding
72. Meritorious
73. Superb
74. Excellent
75. Crackerjack
76. Tip-top
77. Laudable
78. Top-notch
79. Super
80. Amazing
81. Superior
82. Magnificent
83. Superlative
84. Super-duper
85. Skookum
86. Wondrous
87. Fabulous
88. Wonderful
89. Astounding
90. Phenomenal

91. Unreal
92. World-class
93. Stupendous
94. Fantastic
95. Marvellous
96. Peerless
97. Incredible
98. Stupifying
99. Tremendous
100. Supreme
101. Incomparable
102. Unheard of
103. Awesome
104. Brilliant
105. Breathtaking
106. Glorious
107. Best
108. Best ever
109. Mind-blowing
110. Transcendent
111. Perfect
112. Ideal

Transcendent
VII.110

VIII. Is It True?

1. Impossible
2. Unlikely
3. Doubtful
4. Possible
5. Could be
6. Unclear
7. Vague
8. Maybe
9. Probably
10. Seemingly
11. Perceptibly
12. Noticeably
13. Conspicuously
14. Plain
15. Lucidly
16. Evident
17. Manifest
18. Totally
19. Obvious
20. Overt
21. Unmistakable
22. Undeniable
23. Indubitable
24. Unquestionable
25. Undoubted
26. Patently
27. Self-evident

IX. Certainty

1. Impulse
2. Instinct
3. Gut feeling
4. Feeling
5. Emotion
6. Notion
7. Assumption
8. Platitude
9. Idea
10. Proposition
11. Hypothesis
12. Belief
13. Theory
14. Conclusion
15. Conviction
16. Aphorism
17. Tenet
18. Canon
19. Paradigm
20. Proverb
21. Adage
22. Maxim
23. Cardinal paradigm*
24. Truth
25. Axiom
26. Fact

THE HUMAN CORE

I. Introvertedness to Extrovertedness

10-point scale

1. Mute
2. Introverted
3. Quiet
4. Average
5. Open
6. Friendly
7. Outgoing
8. Gregarious
9. Life of the party
10. Raving lunatic

II. Cleverness

1. Imbecilic
2. Moronic
3. Dense
4. Present
5. All-there
6. Alert
7. Witty
8. Sharp
9. Clever
10. Keen
11. Shrewd
12. Cunning
13. Carnegiel*

III. Straight to Gay (Female)

1. Princess
2. Straight
3. Tomboy
4. One time at uni
5. Only when I'm drunk
6. Bi
7. Lipstick lesbian
8. Lesbian
9. Butch
10. Dyke
11. Bull dyke

IV. Straight to Gay (Male)

10-point scale

1. Neanderthal
2. Straight
3. Metero
4. Metro
5. Bi-curious
6. Hetero-flexible
7. Bi
8. Gay
9. Flaming
10. Liberace gay

V. Chastity

1. Nun
2. Celibate
3. Virgin
4. Good girl
5. 'A lady'
6. Flirt
7. Cock tease
8. 'Virgin'
9. Floozy
10. Scandalous
11. Promiscuous
12. Topless dancer
13. Groupie
14. Courtesan
15. Concubine
16. Ho
17. Slut
18. 'Whore'
19. Exotic dancer
20. Stripper
21. High-class call girl
22. Call girl
23. Prostitute
24. Whore
25. Porn star
26. Porn, not a star
27. Cock holster
28. Crack whore
29. Cum dumpster
30. Bukkakee* (note the extra *e*)
31. Gang-bang record holder
32. Your mother

Your Mom
V.32

VI. FAILURE TO SUCCESS

1. Accidentally blinking the universe out of existence
2. Making a black hole in a particle accelerator and destroying the Earth
3. Cataclysmic failure
4. Catastrophic failure
5. FUBAR
6. Munson**
7. Total failure
8. Utter failure
9. Utter disappointment
10. Failure
11. Fuck up
12. Botch
13. Snafu
14. Pwned
15. Loss
16. Disappointment
17. Bare minimum
18. Good enough
19. Competent
20. Honorable mention
21. Accomplishment
22. Success
23. Achievement
24. Win
25. Victory
26. Ovation**
27. Championship
28. Triumph
29. Stamper*

Cordial
VII.18

VII. OFFENSIVE TO CHARMING

1. Repugnant
2. Hateful
3. Mean
4. Offensive
5. Repellant
6. Repulsive
7. Rude
8. Surly
9. Disagreeable
10. Irritating
11. Antisocial
12. Boring
13. Obliging
14. Nice
15. Complaisant
16. Agreeable
17. Kind
18. Cordial
19. Friendly
20. Sweet
21. Sociable
22. Likeable
23. Amiable
24. Pleasant
25. Social
26. Congenial
27. Winsome
28. Enamoring
29. Swell
30. Delightful
31. Charming
32. Graceful
33. Engaging
34. Absorbing
35. Enthralling
36. Magnetizing
37. Fascinating
38. Loveable
39. Engrossing
40. Spellbinding
41. Irresistible
42. Luminescent
43. Scintillating
44. The Face of God

VIII. COOLNESS

1. Schmo
2. Tool
3. Schmuck
4. Putz
5. Nerd
6. Dork
7. Sad
8. A'ight
9. Cool
10. 'In'
11. Hip
12. Studly
13. Popular
14. 'The Shit'
15. Wilderesque*
16. 'It Girl' or 'It Boy'
17. Michael Hatch*

IX. INTELLIGENCE

1. Somatic death
2. Brain-dead
3. Vegetable
4. Profoundly retarded
5. Idiot (clinical)
6. Severely retarded
7. Moderately retarded
8. Cretin
9. Mildly retarded
10. Stupid
11. Slow learner
12. Half-wit
13. Feeble-minded
14. Obtuse
15. Unintelligent
16. Average
17. Together
18. Above average
19. Astute
20. Perceptive
21. Discerning
22. Bright
23. Apt
24. Smart
25. Gifted
26. Genius
27. Whiz
28. Brilliant
29. Perspicacious
30. Prodigy
31. Supercogitative*
32. Universal savant*
33. Hypercogitative*
34. Omnicognisant*

X. RATIONALITY

1. Hysterical
2. Lunatic
3. Insane
4. Psychotic
5. Certifiable
6. Crazy
7. Nuts
8. Under duress
9. Emotional
10. Nutty
11. Unreasonable
12. Subjective
13. Normal
14. Reasonable
15. Stable
16. Level-headed
17. Sensible
18. Stout
19. Logical
20. Prudent
21. Rational
22. Pragmatic
23. Lucid
24. Wise
25. Objective
26. Transcendent

XI. Wisdom

1. Asinine
2. Mad
3. Doltish
4. Daft
5. Foolish
6. Nearsighted
7. Unwise
8. Fatuous
9. Wary
10. Sensible
11. Tactful
12. Prudent
13. Thoughtful
14. Insightful
15. Reflective
16. Intuitive
17. Shrewd
18. Farsighted
19. Wise
20. Sagacious
21. Enlightened
22. Transcendent
23. Omniscien*
24. Omnicien*

Vegetable
IX.3

XII. CONFIDENCE

1. Submissive
2. Obsequious
3. Plebian
4. Supplicatory
5. Proletarian
6. Timorous
7. Withdrawn
8. Diffident
9. Meek
10. Self-effacing
11. Tentative
12. Apprehensive
13. Insecure
14. Timid
15. Self-conscious
16. Hesitant
17. Demure
18. Uncertain
19. Humble
20. Modest
21. Content
22. Ordinary
23. Cool
24. Confident
25. Smug
26. Proud
27. Arrogant
28. Cocky
29. Cavalier
30. Narcissistic
31. Stuck up
32. Haughty
33. Snooty
34. Pretentious
35. Ostentatious
36. Imperious
37. Vainglorious
38. Pompous

XIII. REBELLION TO LOYALTY

1. Mutiny
2. Treachery
3. Perfidy
4. Treason
5. Betrayal
6. Rebellion
7. Defiance
8. Disobedience
9. Disloyalty
10. Passive aggressiveness
11. Passivity
12. Neutrality
13. Adherence
14. Allegiance
15. Loyalty
16. Obedience
17. Fealty
18. Devotion
19. Worship
20. Surrender of free will

XIV. COURAGE

1. Panicky
2. Recreant
3. Craven
4. Dastardly
5. Caitiff
6. Timorous
7. Spineless
8. Cow-hearted
9. Yellow
10. Cowardly
11. Pigeon-hearted
12. Gutless
13. Lily-livered
14. Pusillanimous
15. Fearful
16. Weak-kneed
17. Unmanly
18. Nervous
19. Apprehensive
20. Timid
21. Fainthearted
22. Diffident
23. Shy
24. Bashful
25. Hesitant
26. Approachable
27. Cool
28. Confident
29. Spunky
30. Daring
31. Plucky
32. Gutsy
33. Ballsy
34. Brave
35. Gallant
36. Stout-hearted
37. Courageous
38. Lionhearted
39. Heroic
40. Doughty
41. Valorous
42. Intrepid
43. Valiant
44. Indomitable

Approachable
XIV.26

XV. CREATIVITY

1. Anchor
2. Stale
3. Behind
4. Uninspired
5. Up-to-date
6. Productive
7. Formative
8. Imaginative
9. Creative
10. Inventive
11. Avant-garde
12. Innovative
13. Cutting-edge
14. Ingenious
15. Inspired
16. Dynamic
17. Original
18. Visionary
19. Prolific
20. Demiurgic*
21. True original
22. Edisonian*
23. Protogenor*
24. Protogenoi*

Anchor
XV.1

XVI. Funniness

1. Event horizon
2. Priggish
3. Dreary
4. Puritanical
5. Fusty
6. Prudish
7. Prissy
8. Prim
9. A stick in the mud
10. Staid
11. Humourless
12. Fun sponge
13. Dull
14. Genteel
15. Ordinary
16. Merry
17. Whimsical
18. Blithe
19. Playful
20. Witty
21. Sportive
22. Waggish
23. Amusing
24. Humourous
25. Jolly
26. Funny
27. Droll
28. Jocular
29. Comical
30. Hilarious
31. Side-splitting
32. Hysterical
33. Zazic*
34. Besic*

Whimsical

XVI.17

UNIVERSAL HUMAN EXPERIENCES

I. Degrees of Ultra-Minor Crime

1. Putting a stranger in the spank bank
2. Speeding up on the yellow light
3. Holding a door for a stranger at an awkward distance that requires him to speed up his pace
4. Seeing a well-endowed woman about to pass by you in a crowded room, and leaving your elbow out and pretending not to notice on the off-chance she might brush against it with her boobs
5. Not quickening your pace when a stranger holds the door at an awkward distance
6. Using a student ID when not a student
7. Replacing the TP, but not putting it on the roll
8. Double parking
9. Paying for a water cup, but getting cola
10. Not washing hands (#1)
11. Just rinsing, no soap (#1)
12. Six items in the '5 items or less' queue
13. Not paying for that cola refill
14. Forgetting to put the toilet seat back up
15. Changing the channel while someone else is watching
16. Not replacing the TP
17. Forgetting her name
18. Putting someone on hold for longer than 30 seconds *without* a hold-time estimate
19. Not clearing your table in a clear-your-own table restaurant
20. Putting a friend's girlfriend in the spank bank
21. Tipping badly
22. Taking in a double feature, but paying for just the one
23. Just rinsing, no soap (#2)
24. Not tipping
25. Not washing hands (#2)
26. Littering
27. Spoiling the end of a film
28. Putting someone on hold for longer than a minute *without* a hold-time estimate

II. Challenges

1. Suggestive automation
2. Anticipatory automation
3. Automated
4. Effortless
5. A snap
6. A piece of cake
7. Child's play
8. A cinch
9. Elementary
10. No sweat
11. Like taking candy from a baby
12. Painless
13. Uninvolved
14. Yielding
15. Easy
16. Simple
17. Everyday
18. Manageable
19. Bothersome
20. Difficult
21. Tough
22. Hard
23. Challenging
24. Burdensome
25. Demanding
26. Trying
27. Taxing
28. Exacting
29. Toilsome
30. Operose
31. Immense
32. Arduous
33. Herculean
34. Titanic
35. Unyielding
36. Foolhardy
37. Impossible

No sweat

II.10

III. Degrees of Disaster

1. Faux pas
2. Snafu
3. Pull a Brian*
4. Setback
5. Mishap
6. Flop
7. Disruption
8. Woe
9. Fiasco
10. Pull a Munson** (or To get Munsoned **)
11. Debacle
12. Defeat
13. Gate generator*
14. Emergency
15. Ruining
16. Tragedy
17. Blight
18. Bane
19. Scourge
20. Calamity
21. Disaster
22. Ruination
23. Devastation
24. Index generator*
25. Inundation
26. Catastrophe
27. Desolation
28. Holocaust
29. Decimation
30. Annihilation
31. Cataclysm
32. Extinction event/ extinction-level event
33. Paroxysm
34. Apocalypse
35. Catalypse*
36. Cacolypse*
37. Dipocalypse*
38. Multocalypse*
39. Pluracalypse*
40. Omnocalypse*
41. Pangeaclasm*
42. Pangeacylsm*
43. Pangeocalypse*
44. Geoclasm*
45. Geoclysm*
46. Geocalypse*
47. Alderaan*
48. Geoblink*
49. Solaclasm*
50. Solaclysm*
51. Solacalypse*
52. Solablink*
53. Galactoclasm*
54. Galactoclysm*
55. Galactoclypse*
56. Galactoblink*
57. Branoclasm*
58. Branoclysm*
59. Branocalypse*
60. Branoblink*
61. Bulkoclasm*
62. Bulkoclysm*
63. Bulkalypse*
64. Bulkoblink*
65. Omniblink*

IV. Insult to Praise

1. Damnatio Memoriae*
2. Say the one thing everyone's thinking*
3. Read the riot act
4. Vilify
5. Spew obloquies
6. Hiss
7. Boo
8. Smear
9. Insult
10. Put down
11. Deride
12. Pan
13. Burn
14. Bag
15. Gibe
16. Girb
17. Zing
18. Describe
19. Compliment
20. Praise
21. Extol
22. Laud
23. Panegyrize
24. Sing praise
25. Exalt
26. Glorify
27. Deify
28. Apotheosize
29. Worship

V. Pleasure to Pain

1. Orgasm
2. Euphoria
3. Bliss
4. Titillation
5. Massage
6. Pleasurable touch
7. Human contact
8. Comfort
9. Numbness
10. Tenderness
11. Discomfort
12. Tingle
13. Twinge
14. Irritation
15. Smart
16. Pain
17. Hurt
18. Dolor
19. Ache
20. Searing pain
21. Anguish
22. Torture
23. Causalgia
24. Excruciating pain
25. Torment
26. Unbearable pain
27. Overwhelming pain
28. Agony
29. Passing out from the pain
30. Artificial maltactoplasty*

VI. How Are You Doing?

1. Why SHOULDN'T I jump??!!!
2. Spare change?
3. I am so totally fucked
4. Oh my God, I have had the WORST day
5. I feel like shit
6. Well, it's been a long day
7. OK, I guess
8. OK
9. Just fine
10. Fine
11. Dandy
12. Fine and dandy
13. Great
14. Couldn't be better
15. Great, thanks for asking
16. Oh my God, I have had the BEST day
17. I'm in the zone
18. I feel like I'm on top of the world
19. I feel like I could conquer the world

VII. Hobby Interest

1. Dabbler
2. Tyro
3. Dilettante
4. 'Into'
5. Fan
6. Hobbyist
7. Lover
8. Nut
9. Freak
10. Fanatic
11. Gourmet
12. Connoisseur
13. Bon vivant
14. Cognoscente
15. Aesthete

VIII. Sports Prowess

1. Youth
2. High School Frosh-Soph
3. High School Junior Varsity
4. High School Varsity
5. College
6. Semi-Pro/Farm
7. Pro
8. Pro Starter
9. All-Star
10. Hall of Fame

IX. SEVERITY OF INJURY

1. Nick
2. Prick
3. Stub
4. Strawberry
5. Boo-boo
6. Scrape
7. Stick
8. Sore
9. Bruise
10. Cut
11. Deep bruise
12. Sprain
13. Gouge
14. Stress fracture
15. Gash
16. Fracture
17. Wound
18. Dislocation
19. Concussion
20. Compound fracture
21. Trauma
22. Impalement
23. Massive trauma
24. Disembowelment
25. Dismemberment
26. Profound trauma
27. Decapitation
28. Eeeeewwww ...
29. Hamburger
30. Disintegrated
31. Forgotten
32. Annulled

Nick

IX.1

X. People You'd Want to Be There in a Life-or-Death Emergency Situation

1. Boy scout
2. Lifeguard
3. Auxillary nurse
4. Paramedic
5. Nurse
6. GP
7. A&E doctor
8. A&E consultant

XI. Degrees of Jokes

1. Pun
2. Play on words
3. Knock-knock joke
4. 'Your Mother' joke
5. Well-executed deadpan
6. Works on so many levels
7. A stupid image, video, or act that, when seen again or remembered, elicits unstoppable cycles of giggles
8. The joke God tells you when you get to heaven that keeps you laughing for eternity

XII. Laugh-O-Meter

1. I don't get it
2. Heh
3. Grin
4. Chuckle
5. Chortle
6. Guffaw
7. In stitches
8. Side-splitting
9. Paroxysm
10. Roll in the aisles
11. Chew a lung
12. Die of laughter

XIII. Safe Places to Keep Stuff

1. Behind your socks
2. Under the mattress
3. An old coffee can
4. Locked drawer
5. Locked filing cabinet
6. Buried out back
7. Safe
8. Vault
9. Fort Knox
10. NORAD

XIV. THE SIGNIFICANCE OF EVENTS

1. Inconsequential
2. Couldn't care less
3. Whatever
4. Optional
5. Everyday
6. Noteworthy
7. Red letter day
8. Important
9. Dramatic
10. Newsworthy
11. Remarkable
12. Grandiose
13. Catastrophic
14. Historical
15. Epic
16. Calliopic*
17. Monumental
18. Apolloic
19. Cataclysmic (Biblical)
20. Nuclear
21. Geologic
22. Biblical
23. Golgothic/Bodhic/ Hiric/Sinaic*; epochal/messianic
24. Apocalyptic
25. Cataclysmic (geological)
26. Astronomical
27. Galactic
28. Cosmic
29. Universal
30. Branic*
31. Bulkic*
32. Ultimate

Nurse

x.5

XV. Labour Measured by Degrees of Freedom

1. Slavery
2. Involuntary servitude
3. Convict labour
4. Indentured servant
5. Labourer in a command economy, or communist system
6. Serfdom
7. Tax slavery
8. Sweat shop
9. Living wage
10. Minimum wage with additional circumstantial hardship
11. Minimum wage
12. Closed shop
13. Open shop
14. Payday to payday
15. Career track
16. Employment at will
17. Independent contractor
18. Freelance
19. Self-employed
20. Howard Roark (*The Fountainhead*, Ayn Rand)

XVI. Degrees of Academic Tests

1. Homework
2. Quick quiz
3. Quiz
4. Test
5. Exam
6. Exams that actually count towards your final mark
7. Final exam
8. Dissertation

XVII. Degrees of Academic Achievements

1. Pre-school
2. Primary school
3. First school
4. Middle school
5. High school
6. College
7. University (bachelor's)
8. University (master's)
9. University (doctorate)
10. Postdoctoral
11. Cognoscente*
12. Eruditor*
13. Sophic*

XVIII. DEGREES OF LIFE MILESTONES

In order of importance from least to greatest

1. Birthday
2. Anniversary
3. Sweet 16
4. Driver's licence
5. 21st birthday
6. Third marriage/life partnership ceremony/ordination
7. Graduation (middle/secondary school)
8. Over-the-hill party
9. Coming-of-age ceremony (Bar Mitzvah, Quinceañera, debutante ball, Kovave)
10. Graduation (high school)
11. Second marriage/life partnership ceremony/ordination
12. Graduation (college)
13. Retirement party
14. Graduation (Master's degree)
15. Graduation (doctorate)
16. First marriage/life partnership ceremony/ordination
17. World-class achievement (Nobel Prize, Oscar, Fields Medal, Pulitzer, Olympic Gold Medal, World Cup winner's medal)
18. Coronation/taking presidential oath of office
19. Death and funeral
20. Birth
21. Birth of one's own child
22. Apotheosis

Freelance

XV.18

RELATIONSHIPS

I. Intimate Acts Between Two Consenting Parties

1. Nudge
2. Eye contact
3. Holding hands
4. Kiss of the hand
5. Peck on the cheek
6. Backrub
7. Kiss
8. Massage
9. Making out/kiss with tongues (first base)
10. Grope
11. Heavy petting (second base)
12. Frottage, a.k.a. dry humping
13. Hand job
14. Fingering
15. Blow job (third base)
16. Cunnilingus (third base)
17. Sex (home plate)
18. Anal sex
19. Tossing the salad

II. Sex by Voracity

1. Make sweet, sweet love
2. Make love
3. Do it
4. Have sex
5. Pork
6. Fuck
7. Bang
8. Rail
9. Ravage

III. Relations

Fierce to friendly

1. Fight to the death
2. Fight
3. Push and grapple
4. Shouting match
5. Argument
6. Debate
7. Discuss
8. Talk
9. Confide
10. Make out
11. Fool around
12. Have sex
13. Share simultaneous orgasm

IV. Expressions of Straight-Female-to-Straight-Female Affection

1. Oh hi!
2. Oh, hey, I love those (insert name of article of clothing or accessory)
3. Hug
4. Miss kiss
5. Hug and cheek kiss
6. Straight to cheek kiss
7. Double miss kiss
8. Pillow fight
9. Naked pillow fight
10. Naked pillow fight that breaks down into a full-on orgy

Hug
IV.3

V. Expressions of Straight-Male-to-Straight-Male Affection

1. Up nod
2. Hey, what's up
3. Handshake
4. The Rock
5. Grip → Rock
6. High five
7. Grip → over, under → Rock
8. Grip → over, under → Rock and point followed with 'This guy!'
9. Grip → chest bump
10. Grip → chest bump and hold + back pat
11. Full hug with pats
12. Formal cheek kiss (European only)
13. Formal double cheek kiss (diplomacy, Europe, and the Mob only)
14. Full hug with enthusiastic rubbing of back with open palm (billionaires, drug lords, and Europeans only)
15. Full hug without pats, fast release
16. The drunken 'I love you, mate!'
17. Permanent shotgun
18. Full hug with lean-back, eye contact, and re-hugging
19. Championship dogpile
20. Cheek kiss (limit = 6 per lifetime + 1 per son)
21. Old war comrades' long hug at the graveside of the man who saved both their lives during the Battle of the Bulge, or Marathon, or the skirmish against those Neanderthals over that really nice cave right next to the waterfall that flows into the pool with all the fish

VI. Relationships

1. Single
2. Hookup
3. Friends with benefits
4. Seeing
5. Dating
6. Exclusive
7. Boyfriend/girlfriend
8. Engaged to be engaged, a.k.a. domestic partners
9. Engaged
10. Married

Handshake
v.3

VII. PARTY FORMALITY

1. State wake
2. Solemnization
3. State dinner
4. Débutante ball
5. Gala
6. May ball
7. White-tie ball
8. Military ball
9. Masquerade ball
10. Black-tie ball
11. Lawn social
12. Tea party
13. Ball
14. Dance
15. Charity fundraiser
16. Date party
17. Sorority invitational
18. Fiesta
19. Hoedown
20. Fête
21. Street party
22. Sock hop
23. House party
24. Barbeque
25. Lock and key party
26. Wingding
27. Smoker
28. Shindig
29. Beach party
30. Kegger
31. Free party
32. Key party
33. Rave
34. Binge
35. Multi-kegger
36. Blowout
37. Toga party
38. Stag party/stag night/ bachelor party/ bucks party
39. Squat party
40. Foam party
41. Make-out party
42. Coalition of the willing*
43. Saturnalia
44. Debauch
45. Orgy
46. Bacchanalia/bacchanal
47. Clusterfuck
48. Zero gravity quivering limbsphere
49. Omnigamos*

VIII. DEGREES OF SOCIAL ORDERLINESS

1. Anarchy
2. Hysteria
3. Frenzy
4. Mob
5. Wedding reception
6. Swarm
7. Gang
8. Throng
9. Clump
10. Group
11. Clique
12. Society
13. Courtroom
14. Funeral
15. Wedding
16. Formation
17. State funeral
18. Coronation Mass

Kegger
VII.31

IX. MEETINGS

1. Passing glance
2. Nod
3. Hello/hey/
   what's up?/ hi
4. Handshake
5. Huddle
6. Gathering
7. Meeting
8. Pow-wow
9. Board
10. Council
11. Assembly
12. Conclave
13. House
14. Parliament
15. House of lords
16. Summit
17. Bilderbergoid*
18. Grand Terramot*
19. Apogee*

X. FRIENDSHIP

1. Archnemesis
2. Archenemy
3. Nemesis
4. Enemy
5. Foe
6. Rival
7. I don't want to say any
   thing bad about them
   but ... like ...
8. We don't really get along
9. I don't mind them
10. I've heard of them
11. We've met
12. I know them
13. Acquaintance
14. Buddy
15. Friend
16. Chum
17. Pal
18. Good friend
19. MySpace Top 8,
    off and on
20. Lifelong friend
21. One of my best friends
22. MySpace Top 8
    permanent fixture
23. Usher/bridesmaid
24. Like a brother/sister
    to me
25. Best friend/BFFL
26. BFF
27. Best man/maid of
    honour
28. Godparent of child
29. Platonic life partner

XI. PHYSICAL EXPRESSIONS OF SUBJUGATION

1. Avoiding eye contact
2. Not turning your back
3. Curtsy
4. Ring kiss
5. Bow
6. Kneel
7. Kowtow

Lifelong friend
X.20

EMOTIONS

5

I. SHADES OF ANGER

1. Inert
2. Comatose
3. Stoical
4. Nirvana
5. Pellucid
6. Limpid
7. Halcyon
8. Serene
9. Quiescent
10. Clear
11. Tranquil
12. Pacific
13. Detached
14. Relaxed
15. Phlegmatic
16. Keeping your head when all about you are losing theirs**
17. Stolid
18. Calm
19. Composed
20. Steady
21. Collected
22. Mellow
23. Cool
24. Easy
25. Unruffled
26. Unagitated
27. Unperturbed
28. Impassive
29. Together
30. Alert
31. Nervous
32. Anxious
33. Uptight
34. Displeased
35. Fretful
36. Frustrated
37. Bitter
38. Sullen
39. Huffy
40. Annoyed
41. Grouchy
42. Edgy
43. Ruffled
44. In a bad mood
45. Cranky
46. Testy
47. Snapish
48. Disgruntled
49. Stewed
50. Resentful
51. Touchy
52. Miffed
53. Grumpy
54. Dudgeon
55. Peevish
56. Taking umbrage
57. Chafed
58. Irritated
59. Pettish
60. Nettled
61. In a snit
62. Piqued
63. Roiled
64. Ticked off
65. Driven crazy
66. Agitated
67. Irked
68. Teed off

69. Sore
70. Rankled
71. Vexed
72. Pissed off
73. Irascible
74. Cross
75. Upset
76. Riled
77. Bristling
78. Excited
79. Riled up
80. Mad
81. Worked up
82. Angry
83. Exasperated
84. Galled
85. Fuming
86. Hot under the collar
87. Heated
88. Good and mad
89. Indignant
90. Incensed
91. Burned up
92. Offended
93. Vehement
94. Bent out of shape
95. Terribly vexed**
96. Het up
97. Boiling
98. Ireful
99. Turbulent
100. Irate
101. Ranting and raving
102. Infuriated
103. Overwrought

104. '... a mushroom cloud layin mother-fucker, motherfucker ...' (Jules, *Pulp Fiction*)
105. Furious
106. Enraged
107. Mad as hell
108. Throwing a fit
109. Seeing red
110. Rabid
111. Unglued
112. Flared-up
113. Beside oneself
114. Throwing a tantrum
115. Foaming at the mouth
116. Uncontrollable
117. Possessed
118. Choleric
119. 'I'm mad as hell, and I'm not going to take this anymore!' (Howard Beale, *Network*)
120. Belligerent
121. Going ape
122. Corybantic
123. Violent
124. Storming
125. Virulent
126. Outraged
127. Going ape-shit
128. Fit to be tied
129. Wrathful
130. Tumultuous
131. Tempestuous

132. Convulsed
133. Pitching a
    conniption fit
134. Ferocious
135. Fierce
136. Explosive
137. Fulminatory
138. Apoplectic

139. Volcanic
140. Paroxysmal
141. Rancorous
142. Berserk
143. Nuclear
144. Ultra-Plinian*
145. Jake*

Boiling
1.97

II. Fear Itself

1. Omnipotence combined with omnificence
2. Omnipotence
3. Omnificence
4. Invincibility
5. Invulnerability
6. Immortality
7. Peace of mind
8. Security
9. Safety
10. Hope
11. Anticipation
12. Uncertainty
13. Confusion
14. Doubt
15. Uneasiness
16. Care
17. Restlessness
18. Worry
19. Concern
20. Uneasiness
21. Watchfulness
22. Nervousness
23. Solicitude
24. Disquietness
25. Jitters
26. Apprehension
27. Anxiety
28. Butterflies
29. The heebie jeebies
30. Suspense
31. The shakes
32. Trepidation
33. Goosebumps
34. The willies
35. Foreboding
36. Distress
37. The creeps
38. The all-overs
39. Fear
40. Alarm
41. Dread
42. Cold sweat
43. Fright
44. Panic
45. Horror
46. Scared shitless
47. Terror
48. Shock
49. Petrifaction
50. Sweating blood

III. Shame to Pride

1. Nadiral antrium*
2. Suicidal mortification*
3. Nauseous mortification*
4. Antrium*
5. What have I done??!!
6. Numbing stupefaction*
7. Shameful stupefaction*
8. Opprobrium

9. Mortification
10. Ignominy
11. Shame
12. Odium
13. Rue/ruefulness
14. Repentance
15. Attrition
16. Dishonour
17. Ruth
18. Disgrace
19. Regret
20. Humiliation
21. Contriteness
22. Rejection
23. Penitence
24. Remorse
25. Obloquy
26. Stick your tail between your legs
27. Embarrassment
28. Compunction
29. Discomfiture
30. Chagrin
31. Guilt
32. Resignation
33. Apathy
34. Shrug*
35. Indifference
36. Satisfaction
37. Gratification
38. Self-esteem
39. Self-respect
40. Pride
41. Self-confidence
42. Amour-propre
43. Triumph
44. Like I could conquer the world
45. Glorious
46. Empyrean*
47. Apogeean*
48. Apotheosis
49. Transcendence
50. Humility

Butterflies

II.28

IV. Happiness to Sadness

1. Transported
2. Rapturous
3. In seventh heaven
4. Entranced
5. Glorious
6. Beatitudinous
7. Ecstatic
8. Blessed
9. Felicitous
10. Rhapsodic
11. Flying high
12. Euphoric
13. Ravishment
14. Overjoyed
15. Delirious
16. Mirthful
17. Jubilant
18. Exhilarated
19. Tickled pink
20. Exalted
21. Tellusian*
22. Blissful
23. Elated
24. Joyous
25. Kleobian or Bitonian
26. Enchanted
27. Gay
28. Effervent
29. Gleeful
30. Sunny
31. Delighted
32. Jolly
33. Spirited
34. Cheerful
35. Merry
36. Ebullient
37. Relishing
38. Exuberant
39. Vim
40. Inspired
41. Delectable
42. Vivacious
43. Zestful
44. In high spirits
45. Peppy
46. Enthusiastic
47. Zingy
48. Buoyant
49. Vital
50. Lively
51. Gratified
52. Glad
53. Happy
54. Relieved
55. Light
56. Chipper
57. Pleased
58. Genial
59. In good humour
60. Feeling good
61. Satisfied
62. Snug
63. Relaxed
64. Reposed
65. At ease
66. Content
67. Comfortable
68. Appeased

69. Calm
70. Cool
71. Sufficient
72. Having the ho-hums
73. Apathetic
74. Pessimistic
75. Filled with ennui
76. Dispirited
77. Cheerless
78. Dull
79. Having the blahs
80. In the doldrums
81. Discouraged
82. Saturnine
83. Low
84. Disappointed
85. Having the mopes
86. Bummed
87. Having the blues
88. Dejected
89. In low spirits
90. Unhappy
91. Sad
92. Downhearted
93. Dreary
94. Having the mulligrubs
95. Depressed
96. In a funk
97. Despondent
98. Having the mubblefubbles
99. Melancholy
100. In a blue funk
101. Down in the dumps
102. Dismal
103. Having the blue devils
104. Gloomy
105. Ruthian**
106. Perturbed
107. Abject
108. With a heavy heart
109. Troubled
110. Sorrowful
111. Mourning
112. Woeful
113. Dolorous
114. Grieving
115. Shaken
116. Distressed
117. Miserable
118. Dismayed
119. Brokenhearted
120. Hopeless
121. Wretched
122. Distraught
123. Shattered
124. Despairing
125. Anguished
126. Desperate
127. Inconsolable
128. Clinically depressed
129. In agony
130. Disconsolate
131. Desolate
132. Lugubrious
133. Suicidal

V. Happiness to Sadness, as Expressed in Emoticons

1. :.D
2. :.)
3. =D
4. :D
5. =)
6. :)
7. :P

8. :|
9. :\
10. :s
11. :(
12. :.(
13. D.:

VI. Hollowness to Fulfilment

1. Vacuous
2. Hollow
3. Empty
4. Homesick
5. Lonely
6. Satisfied
7. Fulfilled

8. Replete
9. Self-actualized
10. My cup runneth over
11. Bursting at
    the seams
12. Monk giggly*

=)
v.5

VII. Resentment to Gratitude

1. Vendetta
2. Revenge
3. Resentment
4. Tolerance
5. Acknowledgement
6. Credit
7. Thanks
8. Appreciation
9. Requital
10. Gratitude
11. Indebtedness
12. Gaboprexy*
13. Hypergaboprexy*
14. Innuot*
15. Wannuot*
16. Peduot*
17. Wampoklak*
18. Heepodoo*
19. Fanaticism

VIII. Hate to Love

Degrees of feelings for another

1. Hold rancor
2. Execrate
3. Declare taboo
4. Shun
5. Harbour enmity towards
6. Abhor
7. Hold in odium
8. Hate
9. Despise
10. Loathe
11. Disdain
12. Detest
13. Dislike
14. Disapprove
15. Feel ambivalent towards
16. Associate
17. Approve
18. Like
19. Admire
20. Feel affection for
21. Love
22. Be 'in love with'/ Luff**/Lerve**
23. Adore
24. Deify
25. Worship

IX. ENTHUSIASM

1. The look on the scientists' faces when I show them my perpetual motion machine
2. Fight or flight
3. Revulsion
4. Disgust
5. Antipathy
6. Pity
7. Boredom
8. Ambivalence/ indifference
9. Curiosity
10. Drawn towards
11. Eagerness
12. Passion
13. Enthusiasm
14. Intensity
15. Zeal
16. Lust
17. Fanaticism
18. The look on every- one else's face when I show them my per- petual motion machine

Curiosity
IX.9

X. EMOTION FROM NEGATIVE TO POSITIVE

Admittedly ultra-subjective

1. Rancor
2. Horror
3. Panic
4. Rage
5. Hate
6. Shame
7. Fear
8. Enmity
9. Suffering
10. Self-pity
11. Grief
12. Righteous indignation
13. Melancholia
14. Anger
15. Depression
16. Humiliation
17. Emptiness
18. Regret
19. Rejection
20. Remorse
21. Doubt
22. Bitterness
23. Disgust
24. Loneliness
25. Contempt
26. Homesickness
27. Repentance
28. Disappointment
29. Jealousy
30. Embarrassment
31. Guilt
32. Frustration
33. Envy
34. Shyness
35. Confusion
36. Boredom
37. Anxiety
38. Apathy
39. Pity
40. Calmness
41. Alertness
42. Surprise
43. Anticipation
44. Lust
45. Serenity
46. Acceptance
47. Happiness
48. Gratitude
49. Gratification
50. Affection
51. Pride
52. Enthusiasm
53. Fulfilment
54. Hope
55. Epiphany
56. Love
57. Ecstasy

XI. Intensity of Feeling

1. Comatose
2. Glacial
3. Icy
4. Cold
5. Calculated
6. Controlled
7. Even-keeled

8. Passionate
9. Emotional
10. Intense
11. Id slave*
12. Hysterical
13. Uncontrollable

XII. Surprise!

1. Omnificence
2. Certainty
3. Expectation
4. Anticipation
5. Pleasantly surprised
6. Caught off guard
7. Startled

8. Surprised
9. Shocked
10. 'You almost gave me a heart attack!'
11. Stupefaction
12. Kujanic Ceramicide
13. Mortal shock

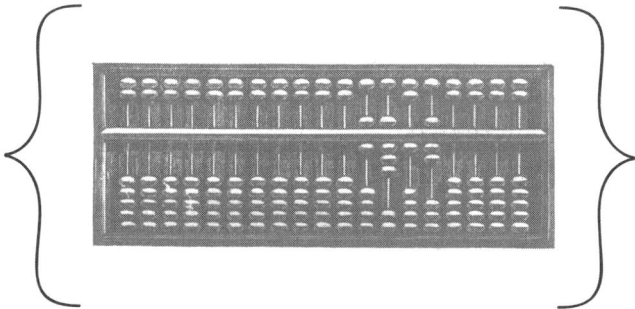

Calculated

XI.5

COMMUNICATION OVERLOAD

I. THE SIZE OF WRITING

1. Ibmigraphy* (IBM writing with atoms)
2. Laser diamond engraving
3. Your name on a grain of rice
4. Mechanical pencil
5. Ballpoint pen
6. Coloured pencil
7. Sharpie
8. Crayon
9. Marker
10. Chalk
11. Giant marker
12. Paint brush
13. Paint roller
14. Billboard
15. Skywriting
16. Crop circles
17. Cloud light projection
18. Obtrusive space billboard
19. Brownic solography* (Frederic Brown's *Pi in the Sky*)
20. Frysolography* (*Futurama*)
21. Supernovagraphy**
22. GRB-ography* (gamma-ray bursts)
23. Galaxography*
24. Cosmography*
25. Branography*
26. Bulkography*
27. Maths

II. HOW SURE ARE YOU?

1. I have absolutely no idea
2. I have no fucking clue
3. I'm completely lost
4. I'm not really sure
5. Well, I don't know …
6. Perhaps …
7. Um …
8. Maybe
9. Probably?
10. Probably
11. I think so
12. Yeah, definitely
13. I'm certain
14. I know it for sure
15. Look, it says it right here …
16. I'm absolutely certain
17. I've never been more sure of anything in my entire life
18. I'd bet my life on it
19. I'd bet your life on it
20. I'd bet my soul on it
21. I'd bet your soul on it

III. SO, HERE'S THE PLAN ... DEGREES OF SANITY OF PLANS AND SCHEMES

1. Impossible
2. Won't work in a million years
3. If you really think you can just waltz in here and ...
4. You're out of your mind!
5. Brave, but stupid
6. Foolhardy
7. Harebrained scheme
8. Cunning plan
9. Just crazy enough to work
10. A regular-brained scheme
11. The best-laid plans
12. Scheme
13. Impromptu idea
14. Master plan

If you really think you can just waltz in here and ...

III.3

1. Vile
2. Outrageous
3. Offensive
4. Horrible
5. More harm than good
6. Ineffectual/useless/zero sum/feckless/purposeless/good-for-nothing
7. Terrible
8. Paltry
9. Awful
10. Inept
11. Maladroit
12. Poor
13. Disappointing
14. Amateurish
15. Inferior
16. Mediocre
17. Competent
18. Ordinary
19. Common
20. Unexceptional
21. Good
22. Peachy
23. Fine
24. Noticeable
25. Well
26. Impressive
27. First-rate
28. Remarkable
29. Textbook
30. Premium
31. Ept*
32. Special
33. Singular
34. Dilly
35. Adroit
36. Praiseworthy
37. Splendid
38. Great
39. Terrific
40. Super
41. Primo
42. Excellent
43. Superb
44. Bang-up
45. Superior
46. Crack
47. Exceptional
48. Outstanding
49. Top-drawer
50. Amazing
51. Fabulous
52. Extraordinary
53. Fantastic
54. Wonderful
55. Marvellous
56. Tremendous
57. Out-of-the-park
58. Grand-slam
59. Astonishing
60. Luminous
61. Spectacular
62. Awesome/awe-inspiring
63. Brilliant
64. Magnificent
65. Astounding
66. Bewildering
67. Breathtaking

68. Phenomenal
69. Incredible
70. Uncanny
71. Stupendous
72. Genius
73. Apprentic*
74. Staggering
75. Glorious
76. Meteoric
77. World-class
78. Stunning
79. Epic
80. Superhuman
81. Supercampian*
82. Inconceivable
83. Unreal
84. Once-in-a-generation
85. Mind-blowing
86. Once-in-a-lifetime
87. Out-of-this-world
88. Blinding
89. Impossibly good
90. Paragonic*
91. Miraculous
92. Preternatural
93. Scary
94. Unsurpassed
95. Legendary
96. Other-worldly
97. Messianic
98. Godlike
99. Divine
100. Perfect
101. Ideal

Bang-up
IV.44

V. THE OBSCENITY CONTINUUM

1. Darn
2. Damn
3. Ass
4. Dick
5. Pussy
6. Cock
7. Shit
8. Fuck
9. Cunt
10. Ethnic-specific term with negative connotation

VI. LIST OF DEMANDS

1. Obsecrate
2. Conjure
3. Besiege
4. Supplicate
5. Implore
6. Crave
7. Beg
8. Importune
9. Plead
10. Sue (old definition)
11. Beseech
12. Pray
13. Petition
14. Nag
15. Woo
16. Advocate
17. Obtest
18. Requisition
19. Entreat
20. Apply
21. Submit
22. Solicit
23. Request
24. Recommend
25. Ask
26. Bid
27. Challenge
28. Lean on
29. Press
30. Charge
31. Urge
32. Insist
33. Oblige
34. Clamour
35. Compel
36. Demand
37. Command
38. Order
39. Coerce
40. Extort
41. Arrogate
42. Force
43. Make
44. Possess

1. Dead
2. Internal paddles
3. Paddles
4. 200 cc's of nitroglycerine
5. Slap in the face
6. Shoulder shake
7. Snap out of it!
8. Pull it together!
9. Are you with me?
10. Good
11. Now focus
12. I think it's cool
13. Relax
14. Put your feet up
15. Rest easy
16. Don't worry
17. Spider-sense ... tingling
18. Um, look ...
19. Caution
20. Are you sitting?
21. Warning
22. You'd better sit down
23. We have a situation
24. Danger
25. Life-or-death situation
26. Use of lethal force authorized
27. Watch out!
28. Look out!
29. Duck!
30. Take cover!
31. Hit the deck!
32. Make your peace with God
33. Pray
34. We're all gonna die!
35. OH SHIT!
36. ... ohh shit
37. Mother of God
38. No.
39. Holy Living Fuck!**

Are you sitting?
VII.20

---

1. Matchbox scribble
2. Napkin doodle
3. 3x5 card
4. Business card
5. Flyer
6. Clipboard
7. Brochure
8. Notes
9. Pamphlet
10. Memorandum
11. Paper
12. Dossier
13. White paper
14. Comic book
15. Research paper
16. Magazine
17. Newspaper
18. News magazine
19. Booklet
20. Handbook
21. Published article
22. Graphic novel
23. Novella
24. Thesis
25. Novel
26. Manifesto
27. Dissertation
28. Compendium
29. Omnibus
30. Volume
31. Encyclopedia
32. Arch-thesis*
33. Treatise
34. Bible
35. Tome
36. Codex
37. Arch-treatise*
38. Arch-Bible*
39. Arch-tome*
40. Arch-codex*
41. Encyclopedia Galactica**
42. Supreme Taxonomy*
43. Lapladex*

Volume

VIII.30

IX. How Bad Do You Want It?

1. Get that shit away from me
2. I wouldn't touch that with a 10-foot pole
3. No way
4. That's not for me
5. No thanks
6. I'm cool
7. Eh
8. I mean, well, if you don't want it, then I guess I'll, um ...
9. Well, I'd hate to see it go to waste ...
10. Oh, sure, what the hell ...
11. Ok, I'll take it
12. I want it
13. I need it
14. Really bad
15. My kingdom for a ...
16. Gimme gimme gimme!
17. Desperately
18. Puhleeeeeze!
19. I'd give anything for it
20. Yes, anything
21. I'm begging you
22. OK, seriously, look, I'm actually on my knees
23. I'd do anything for it
24. Well, not anything
25. OK, yes, anything
26. I'd give my life for it
27. I'd trade my soul for it

I'm begging you
IX.21

X. Degrees of Disaster by Newsworthiness

1. Bad hair day
2. Broken nail
3. Locked out of car
4. Lost mobile
5. Lost keys
6. Lost wallet
7. Getting towed
8. Lost Blackberry
9. Getting audited
10. Getting fired
11. Getting dumped
12. Crash
13. Death
14. Murder-suicide
15. Head-on collision
16. Pile up
17. Collapse
18. Tornado
19. Plane crash
20. Flood
21. Battle
22. Cratering impact
23. Volcano
24. Campaign
25. Pogrom
26. Earthquake
27. War
28. Plague
29. Epidemic
30. Tsunami
31. Scabland generator*/ Augscab*/Missoula flood/ Spokane flood/Bretz flood
32. Impact winter
33. Polarity switch
34. World war
35. Pandemic
36. Limited nuclear exchange
37. Conventional superpower conflict
38. Ecophagy
39. Nuclear exchange
40. Ice age
41. Mass extinction/ Chicxulub/boundary impact
42. Snowball planet
43. Armageddon
44. Crust tsunami
45. Catastrophic disruption
46. Augmark*
47. Local supernova
48. Galaxy gobbling
49. Von Neumann omniclasm*
50. Universal gravitational collapse
51. Bulk ocean nullification*
52. Annihilation of reality*/The Dreaming God awakes
53. The Dreaming God awakes, then forgets what He/She was dreaming about
54. Nullification of reality*

XI. PREFIX HYPERBOLE

Note: Metric prefixes behave differently here, not necessarily attached to a numerical value but rather wielding a certain 'oomph'

1. Anti-
2. Contra-
3. Nulli-
4. Micro-
5. Mini-
6. Mero-
7. Quasi-
8. Semi-
9. Demi-
10. Equi-
11. Extra-
12. Duo-
13. Supra-
14. Arch-
15. Super-
16. Super-duper-
17. Buku-
18. Mega-
19. Hyper-
20. Giga-
21. Ultra-
22. Behemo-
23. Titano-
24. Gygo-*
25. Jorga-*
26. Ragna-*
27. Atma-*,**
28. Ulti-
29. Omni-
30. Meta-

XII. INSTANT MESSENGER LAUGHS

1. ...
2. eh
3. heh
4. ha
5. hah
6. haha
7. lol
8. Lol
9. LOL
10. LOL!
11. LOLOLOL
12. LOLLOLOOOLLAS DFSDFlfdsjkalhk!!!!!
13. LMAO
14. LMFAO
15. ROFL
16. Roflcopter
17. ROFLMAO
18. ROFLMFAO

XII. Talkativeness

1. Omertic*
2. Mute
3. Eremitic
4. Silent
5. Smithmouthed*
6. Muted
7. Muzzled
8. Zipped
9. Mum
10. Speechless
11. Clammed up
12. Tight-lipped
13. Close-mouthed
14. Tongue-tied
15. Nonvocal
16. Wordless
17. Offish/standoffish
18. Terse
19. Chan
20. Curt
21. Silentious
22. Icy
23. Taciturn
24. Sparing
25. Withdrawn
26. Mousy
27. Dour
28. Bashful
29. Reticent
30. Curbed
31. Shy
32. Sedate
33. Diffident
34. Reserved
35. Demure
36. Quiet/quiescent
37. Laconic
38. Distant
39. Communicable
40. Conversable
41. Affable
42. Outgoing
43. Talkative
44. Communicative
45. Talky
46. Gregarious
47. Windy
48. Copious
49. Chatty
50. Yacking/yaky
51. Wordy
52. Gabby
53. Verbose
54. Burbling
55. Voluble
56. Jabbering
57. Profuse
58. Burbly
59. Garrulous
60. Loquacious
61. Long-winded
62. Prolix
63. Gushing
64. Mouthy

65. Multiloquent
66. Motormouth
67. Moschitic*
68. Turbinemouth*

69. Rocketmouth*
70. Niagaric*
71. Tuckerishesqulentness*

XIV. How Welcome You Are

1. Um, can I help you?
2. C'mon in, make yourself
   at home

Muzzled
XIV.7

THE PHYSICAL BODY

I. Digits in Order of Expendability

1. Little toe
2. #4 toe
3. #3 toe
4. #2 toe
5. Pinkie
6. Ring finger
7. Middle finger
8. Big toe/great toe/hallux
9. Index finger
10. Thumb
11. Penis

II. Breast Size

1. Mosquito bite
2. Tittles
3. Miglins
4. Nuglins
5. Titties
6. Tits
7. Boobs
8. Hooters
9. Perfect
10. Melons
11. Gazongas
12. Boulders

III. Penis Size (It Does Matter)

1. Clitoris
2. Peepee
3. Willie
4. Prick
5. Schlort
6. Wand
7. Weiner
8. Ding-dong
9. Penis
10. Wang
11. Dick
12. Johnson
13. Package
14. Cock
15. Schlong
16. Meat
17. Slab
18. Thud
19. Third leg

IV. Physical Fitness

1. Beached whale
2. Elephantine
3. Morbidly obese
4. Adipose
5. Hypertrophied
6. Corpulent
7. Obese
8. Ponderous
9. Wide Load
10. Roly-poly
11. Rotund
12. Tubby
13. Round
14. Bloated
15. Heavy
16. Chunky
17. Pudgy
18. Blowsy
19. Pursy
20. Fat
21. Beer-bellied
22. Weighty
23. Plump
24. Portly
25. Chubby
26. Rubenesque
27. Porcine
28. Swollen
29. Thickset
30. Stocky
31. Heavy-set
32. Weighty
33. Husky
34. Broad-in-the-beam
35. Overweight
36. Well-fed
37. Stout
38. Pleasantly plump
39. Paunchy
40. Pot-bellied
41. Out of shape
42. Able-bodied
43. Average
44. Lean
45. In shape
46. Trim
47. Lithe
48. Fit
49. Strong
50. Muscular
51. Brawny
52. Buff
53. Burly
54. Svelte
55. Ripped
56. Yolked
57. Herculean
58. Schwarzeneggerian*

V. Female Physical Attractiveness

With 10-point scale

1. Two-arm coyote
2. Coyote ugly
3. Yeti with tail (1)
4. Grotesque
5. Yeti
6. Hideous
7. Disgusting
8. Beastly (2)
9. Orca
10. Nasty
11. Beat (3)
12. Ugly (4)
13. Homely
14. 'Eh ...'
15. OK-ish (5)
16. OK
17. Plain (6)
18. Alright
19. Three-beer girl (7)
20. Totally doable
21. Pretty
22. Cute (7.5)
23. Beautiful (8)
24. Fine
25. Sexy
26. Hot (9)
27. 'I wouldn't kick her out of bed'
28. So hot
29. Hot as balls
30. WOW
31. Model hot
32. Gorgeous
33. 'She'll do' (sarcastic)
34. Stunning
35. 'I'd give my left nut'
36. Drop-dead gorgeous
37. Hollywood gorgeous
38. Supermodel
39. '10' (10)

VI. Male Physical Attractiveness

1. Ugly
2. Normal
3. Just a friend
4. Cute
5. Handsome
6. Hot
7. Gorgeous
8. Brad Pitt
9. Adonis

VII. MALE PHYSICAL ATTRACTIVENESS

Alternate funny version

1. Just a friend
2. Dateable
3. Rebound-able
4. One-night-stand-able
5. Cheatworthy

Just a friend

VII.1

VIII. Adorableness of Babies

1. Baby xenomorph
   (from *Alien*)
2. Baby housefly
3. Baby marsupial
4. Baby snake
5. Baby pig
6. Baby cat
7. Baby dog
8. Baby human
9. Baby Ewok
10. Boy band

IX. Amount of Sleep

1. Wink
2. Power nod
3. Power nap
4. Afternoon nap
5. REM cycle
6. A good night's rest
7. Sleep like the dead
8. Coma
9. Permanent vegetative
   state
10. The Big Sleep

X. Burp

1. Hiccup
2. Burp
3. Belch

XI. Magnitude of Flatulence

1. Silent but deadly
2. Pass gas
3. Break wind
4. Fart
5. Let one off
6. Cut the cheese
7. Rip one
8. Follow through
9. Braighetoriate*

Toddler

XIII.11

INGESTION

I. Disgusting to Delicious

1. Leachatic*
2. Coprophagian*
3. Effluvious*
4. Soylent*
5. Putrid
6. Rancid
7. Miikean*
8. Repugnant
9. Vile
10. Revolting
11. Disgusting
12. Nasty
13. Foul
14. Offensive
15. Gross
16. Yucky
17. Icky
18. Grody
19. Yeechy
20. Unpalatable
21. Edible
22. Tasteless
23. Insipid
24. Bland
25. Unsavoury
26. Vapid
27. Unappetizing
28. Flavourless
29. Flat
30. Palatable
31. Appetizing
32. Agreeable
33. Aperitive
34. Good
35. Saporous
36. Yummy
37. Flavoursome
38. Tasty
39. Delish
40. Toothsome
41. Delicious
42. Sapid
43. Scrumptious
44. Mouthwatering
45. Delectable
46. Rich
47. Magnificent
48. Exquisite
49. Savoury
50. Choice
51. Succulent
52. Piquant
53. Heavenly
54. Ambrosial
55. Ichorous*
56. Divine

II. Degrees of Self-Proclaimed Restaurant Notoriety

1. World Famous

III. Meal Size

1. Whiff
2. Crumb
3. Taste
4. Soupçon
5. Peck
6. Nibble
7. Morsel
8. Bite
9. Bonnes Bouches
10. Mouthful
11. Sample
12. Appetizer
13. Something to take the edge off
14. Snack
15. Course
16. Collation
17. Refection
18. Repast
19. Meal
20. Full meal
21. Square meal
22. Blue plate
23. Hearty meal
24. Dinner
25. Table d'hôte/ prix fixe
26. Potluck
27. Feast
28. Banquet
29. Smorgasbord
30. Regale
31. Gorgy*
32. Guinnessack*
33. End Times banquet

IV. Times to Eat

1. Farm breakfast
2. Breakfast
3. Second breakfast
4. Brunch
5. Elevenses
6. Tiffin
7. Lunch
8. Afternoon snack
9. High tea
10. Tea
11. Dinner
12. Supper
13. Late dinner
14. Dessert
15. Late-night snack
16. Midnight snack
17. Kip*
18. Run
19. Dead-of-night bite*

V. Flat Circular Bread

1. Mini Ritz
2. Host wafer/Eucharistic wafer
3. Ritz cracker
4. Pringle
5. Waffle
6. Pancake
7. Pita
8. Tortilla
9. Naan

VI. Ringed Bread

1. Cheerio
2. Mini bagel
3. Mini doughnut
4. Bagel
5. Doughnut
6. Angel food cake
7. Braided round party-sub bread

VII. Fast Food Burger Joint by Burger Quality

1. Wimpy
2. McDonald's
3. Burger King

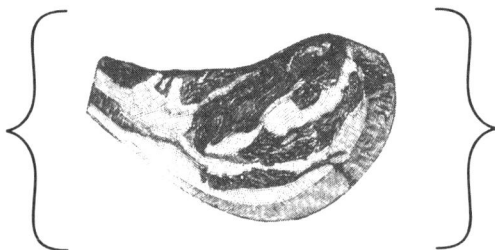

Raw

VIII.2

VIII. How Would You Like Your Steak?

1. Mooing
2. Raw
3. Very rare, a.k.a. blue rare
4. Rare
5. Medium rare
6. Medium
7. Medium well
8. Well done
9. Charcoal

IX. Chocolate Bar Sizes

1. Mini 'M'
2. An 'M'
3. Mini
4. Bite Size
5. Fun Size
6. Bar
7. King Size
8. 200g Bar
9. Emperor Size*

X. Beer Containers by Volume

1. Sip
2. Drink
3. Gulp
4. Shot glass
5. Sampler glass
6. Standard party cup
7. Pint glass
8. Tall glass
9. Half-yard glass
10. Weak beer bong
11. 22, a.k.a. tallboy, a.k.a. tall can
12. Stein
13. Yard glass
14. Proper beer bong
15. Six pack
16. Twelve pack
17. Case
18. Thirty pack
19. Pony keg
20. Keg
21. Barrel
22. Truck
23. Fermenting vat
24. Brewery

XI. BLENDER SETTINGS

1. Ice breaker
2. Pulse
3. Beat
4. Mix
5. Purée
6. Chop
7. Shred
8. Grade
9. Grind
10. Aerate
11. Whip
12. Crumb
13. Blend
14. Frappé
15. Liquefy

XII. ALCOHOL CONTAINERS BY VOLUME

1. Cap
2. Shot
3. Double
4. Flask
5. Bottle
6. Handle

XIII. HOW MANY PEOPLE COULD GET DRUNK FROM ... ?

1. Serving of rum cake
2. One liqueur-filled chocolate
3. Pint of beer/glass of wine/shot of liquor
4. 22, a.k.a. tall boy, a.k.a. tall can
5. Six pack
6. Twelve pack
7. Case of beer
8. Twenty four pack
9. Handle
10. Pony keg
11. Keg
12. Barrel of wine
13. Barrel of whiskey
14. Giant fermenting vat
15. Distillery

XIV. Manliness of Drink

1. Shirley Temple
2. Pepsi Max
3. Daiquiri
4. Blossom Hill
5. Bacardi Breezer
6. WKD
7. Cosmopolitan
8. Standard light beer/lager (Coors Light, Bud Light, Carling C2, etc.)
9. Corona
10. Rum and Coke
11. Standard beer/lager (Stella, Fosters, etc.)
12. Guinness
13. Shots!
14. Dirty martini
15. Martini extra dry
16. Straight vodka
17. Scotch on the rocks
18. Straight bourbon
19. Real ale
20. Everclear

Shirley Temple
XIV.I

XV. Beer Delivery Vehicles

1. Upturned cap
2. Shot glass
3. Sampler glass
4. Can
5. Bottle
6. Standard party cup
7. Pint glass
8. Stein
9. Shotgun
10. Beer bong
11. Super beer bong
12. Truck
13. Freight train
14. Container ship
15. Converted oil tanker

XVI. Degrees of Drunkenness

1. Sober
2. Sober as a priest
   on Sunday
3. Mellow
4. Relaxed
5. Loose
6. Merry
7. Intoxicated
8. Drunk
9. Hit
10. Twisted
11. Pissed
12. Loaded
13. Pissed up
14. Sloshed
15. Fucked up
16. Trashed
17. Smashed
18. Blottoed
19. Gone
20. Sloppy
21. Plastered
22. Blacked out
23. Done
24. Wasted
25. Hammered
26. Dead drunk
27. Obliterated
28. Crawling
29. Shitfaced
30. Hospitalized
31. Comatose
32. Dead

1. Chicken soup
2. Lack of sleep
3. Cabin fever
4. Sugar
5. Chocolate
6. Aspirin
7. Caffeine
8. Alcohol
9. Nicotine
10. Marijuana
11. Mushrooms

12. Ecstasy
13. Laughing gas
14. Speed
15. Coke
16. Special K
17. LSD
18. Crystal meth
19. Opium
20. Crack
21. Heroin
22. Happy Button*

Stein
xv.8

THE ORGANS OF CULTURE

I. You're Cool or a Geek If What You Do for Fun Is …

1. Your multiple live-in Playboy Playmate girl-friends, at 80+ years old
2. Simultaneous multiple A-list actresses
3. Multiple A-list actresses
4. A-list actresses
5. Supermodels
6. Other celebrities
7. Models
8. Cheerleaders
9. Go out
10. Play sports
11. Work out
12. Play poker
13. Watch sports
14. Watch *Star Wars*
15. Watch *Lord of the Rings*
16. Watch poker
17. Read comic books
18. Read *Lord of the Rings*
19. Watch *Star Trek*
20. Write code
21. Play *Dungeons & Dragons*
22. Hack
23. Be the dungeon master (DM)
24. Gripe about 'universe continuity' (comics, sci-fi, etc.)
25. Attend conventions (in the same order of precedence)
26. Go to the historical reinactment
27. Live-action roleplaying
28. Attend conventions in costume (in the same order of precedence)
29. Live-action roleplaying DM
30. Work at the historical reinactment
31. Write and release computer worms and viruses (A special message just for them: Fuck you, you time-sucking, life-interrupting, stranger-hurting, malevolent, vindictive, malignant, appendix-of-civilization, vile, smirking piece of shit. You make other people's lives worse.)

II. Progression of Music

1. Note	6. Ballad
2. Beat	7. Album
3. Refrain	8. Concerto
4. Verse	9. Symphony
5. Song	10. Opus

III. Theatre Audience Reaction

1. Lynching in the street by an angry mob
2. Violently chasing off the stage
3. Launching tomatoes
4. Getting up to leave in protest
5. Repeat heckling
6. Some guy yelling, 'Get off the stage!'
7. Booing
8. Eye-rolling
9. Looking bored
10. Neutral
11. Attentively listening
12. Scattered clapping
13. Clapping
14. Applauding
15. Standing ovation
16. Extended standing ovation demanding multiple curtain calls
17. Rolling in the aisles/ sobbing/cheering
18. Carrying out into the streets on the shoulders of adoring fans

IV. DEGREES OF FUNNY BROTHERS

1. Wachowski
2. Mario
3. Baldwin
4. Wilson
5. Smothers
6. Coen
7. Farrelly
8. Wayans
9. Zucker
10. Marx

V. COMEDIAN PRESTIGE

1. I've thought about doing stand-up
2. MySpace.com comedy video posted
3. Open mic at a minor stage
4. Open mic at the Comedy Store/Jongleurs
5. Regular at a minor stage
6. Regular at the Comedy Store/Jongleurs
7. Own stand up show
8. Appearance on the Royal Variety Show
9. Major TV sitcom
10. Big movie deal

VI. MOVIE RATINGS

1. Uc
2. U
3. PG
4. 12A
5. 12
6. Softcore
7. X
8. 18
9. Porn
10. XX
11. R18
12. XXX
13. Hardcore
14. Gang bang
15. Bukkake
16. Extreme fetish-specific
17. Sheize
18. Snuff

VII. MOVIE SCALE

From Intimate to Epic

1. Internal: *The Sound and the Fury*
2. Intimate: *Ordinary People*
3. Ecclectic: *In Good Company, The Royal Tenenbaums*
4. Sport: *Rocky, Mighty Ducks*
5. Action: *Speed, Airplane!, Bond*
6. Epic: *Mission: Impossible, Pirates of the Caribbean*
7. Sweeping: *Braveheart, Gladiator, Lord of the Rings*
8. Calliopic: *Armageddon, Independence Day, Fifth Element*
9. Apolloic: *Star Wars, Crisis on Infinite Earths*
10. Ultimate: *Ragnarok, Titanomachy, The Great Beyond*

Marx

IV.10

1. Grunt
2. Minion
3. Hustler
4. Goon
5. Thug
6. Henchman
7. Gangsta
8. Pirate
9. Captain Q*
10. Gang leader
11. Gangster
12. Wise guy
13. Made man
14. The Clicker*
15. Pirate captain
16. Consiglieri
17. Boss
18. Mad scientist
19. Corporate baddy
20. Godfather
21. Kingpin
22. Evil genius
23. Evil sorcerer/wizard/conjurer/warlock
24. Generalissimo
25. Tyrant
26. Evil emperor
27. Führer
28. Malithogog*
28. Brain Bug/Zerg Overmind/Borg Queen, etc.**
29. Focal antagonistic deity
30. Evil god

Wizard

VIII.23

IX. Mafia Movie by Quality

1. *The Godfather Part III*
2. *The Untouchables*
3. *Scarface*
4. *The Departed*
5. *Miller's Crossing*
6. *Goodfellas*
7. *Casino*
8. *The Godfather Part I* and *Part II*

X. Alien Movie by Quality

1. *Mac and Me*
2. *Mars Attacks!*
3. *Independence Day*
4. *Alien*
5. *E.T.*

XI. Sci-Fi Universe by Nerd Aroma

Least Nerdy to Most

1. *Independence Day*
2. *The Terminator*
3. *Starship Troopers*
4. *Doctor Who* (new)
5. *Alien*
6. *The Matrix*
7. *Star Wars*
8. *Stargate*
9. *Star Trek: The Next Generation*
10. *Firefly*
11. *StarCraft*
12. *Star Trek* original TV series
13. *Babylon 5*
14. *Doctor Who* (old)
15. *Foundation*
16. *Spelljammer*

XII. Fantasy Medievalish Universe by Nerd Aroma

Least Nerdy to Most

1. Robin Hood
2. Arthurian legend
3. *Zelda*
4. *Final Fantasy*
5. *Warcraft*
6. *The Lord of the Rings*
7. *Narnia*
8. *Magic: The Gathering*
9. *Dungeons & Dragons*

XIII. DEGREES OF NORMAL AND STRANGE

1. Constant
2. Perpetual
3. Inevitable
4. Absolute
5. Certain
6. Extropic*
7. Inveterate
8. Predictable
9. Ritual
10. Orthodox
11. Tralatitious
12. Iterative
13. Traditional
14. Decorous
15. Run-of-the-mill
16. Mundane
17. Routine
18. Matter-of-course
19. Generic
20. Vanilla
21. Wonted
22. Expected
23. Clichéd
24. Entopic
25. Conventional
26. Regular
27. Customary
28. Humdrum
29. Typical
30. Normal
31. Usual
32. General
33. Garden variety
34. Likely
35. Plain
36. Common
37. Familiar
38. Unexceptional
39. Uneventful
40. Unremarkable
41. Unwonted
42. Unorthodox
43. Unconventional
44. Uncustomary
45. Atypical
46. Unlikely
47. Unusual
48. Funny
49. Different
50. Heteromorphic
51. Foreign
52. Irregular
53. Unexpected
54. Out-of-the-way
55. Odd
56. Queer
57. Uncommon
58. Offbeat
59. Curious
60. Novel
61. Idiosyncratic
62. Screwy
63. Peculiar
64. Fishy
65. Outlying
66. Heteroclite
67. Exotic
68. Exceptional
69. Unfamiliar
70. Strange

71. Abnormal
72. Weird
73. Remarkable
74. Deviant
75. Anomalous
76. Aberrant
77. Alien
78. Ectopic
79. Extraordinary
80. Bizarre
81. Far-out
82. Freakish
83. Plausible
84. Outlandish
85. Phenomenal
86. Outré
87. Ridiculous
88. Anachronistic
89. Fantastic
90. Implausible
91. Incredible

92. Uncanny
93. Surreal
94. Ludicrous
95. Unheard of
96. Preternatural
97. Boggling
98. Unearthly/unworldly
99. Phantasmagoric
100. Unimaginable/ unthinkable
101. Otherworldly
102. Transcendental
103. Incogitable/ inconceivable
104. Supersensory/ unknowable
105. Supergodly*
106. Superreal*
107. Impossible
108. Grakkaw*

Freakish
XIII.82

XIV. Degrees of Explosion

1. Decay of an electron
2. Spark
3. Lick
4. Flame
5. Fire
6. Flash
7. Pop
8. Bang
9. Boom
10. Combustion
11. Detonation
12. Explosion
13. Vulcanian eruption (Volcanic Explosivity Index: Severe)
14. Fission Bomb
15. Hydrogen Bomb
16. Plinian eruption (VEI: Cataclysmic)
17. Krakatoan eruption (VEI: Super-colossal)
18. Toban eruption (VEI: Mega-colossal)
19. Planet killer
20. Kryptonian geoclasm
21. Supernova
22. Gamma-ray burst
23. The Big Bang
24. Augreal*

XV. Things That Crush Things Good

1. Nutcracker
2. Crab-leg crusher
3. Molar
4. Can crusher
5. Garbage compactor
6. Vise
7. Steamroller
8. Pneumatic press
9. Car crusher
10. The Mariana Trench
11. Tectonic plates
12. A pair of the largest possible solid planets colliding with big giant diamond plates on them for better smashing
13. Neutron star
14. Black hole (information preserved)
15. Black hole (information not preserved)
16. Brane collision point
17. Mariana-like trench at the bottom, or centre, or whichever is denser, of the hypothetical brane-bubble ocean

XVI. Things That Pry Things Good

1. Toothpick
2. Fingernail
3. Pocketknife
4. Bottle opener
5. Screwdriver

6. Oyster knife
7. Claw of a hammer
8. Crowbar
9. Neighbour
10. Defense attorney

Defense attorney
XVI.10

XVII. Things That Smash Things Good

1. Flyswatter
2. Newton's cradle
3. Reflex hammer
4. Rolled-up newspaper
5. Hand
6. Mallet
7. Paddle
8. Hammer
9. 2x4
10. Baseball bat
11. Club
12. Mace
13. Sledgehammer
14. Battering ram
15. Piling driver
16. Wrecking ball
17. Trireme
18. Meteor
19. Asteroid
20. Dwarf planet
21. Planet
22. Largest possible planet while remaining solid and not getting all lame and gaseous like Jupiter and Saturn

XVIII. Degrees of Villain Hubris

1. Mwuhahahaha!!!
2. Excellent ...
3. Good, just as I planned
4. There is no escape; my plan is foolproof
5. It's no matter, let's just see how they handle my (army of robots, kung-fu warriors, flying monkeys, etc.)
6. What do you mean they've defeated my (army of robots, kung-fu warriors, flying monkeys, etc.)?!???!!!
7. Guards! Seize them!
8. Fools!
9. You're bluffing
10. I don't believe you
11. You don't have what it takes to kill me
12. Curses!
13. Blast!
14. Impossible
15. It can't be
16. No
17. Impossible!
18. It can't be!!!
19. NOOOOOOOOOOO!!!!!
20. Whyyy?!!!!
21. Aaaaaarrrgghhh!!!

XIX. Degrees of 'Living Disabled' Monsters

1. Zombie
2. Spook
3. Ghost
4. Vampire
5. Spectre
6. Fiend
7. Demon
8. Devil

XX. The Cartoon Hierarchy of Intimidation

1. Mouse
2. Cat
3. Dog
4. Lion
5. Elephant
6. Mouse

XXI. Video Game Prowess and/or Difficulty Settings

1. Noob
2. Pwnee
3. Rookie
4. Beginner
5. Amateur
6. Intermediate
7. Advanced
8. Professional
9. Expert
10. l337
11. Ace
12. Champion
13. Master
14. Legend
15. God-like
16. Suicide
17. Impossible

Mouse

xx.1, xx.6

CONSUMER AFFAIRS

I. Personal Wealth

1. Refugee
2. Homeless
3. Indigent
4. Destitute
5. Beggared
6. Needy
7. Impoverished
8. Bankrupt
9. Stone broke
10. Flat broke
11. Impecunious
12. Poverty-stricken
13. Poor
14. Strapped
15. Lower-class
16. Lower middle-class
17. Comfortable
18. Middle-class
19. Upper middle-class
20. Well-off
21. 'Comfortable'
22. Upper-class
23. Rich
24. Millionaire
25. Multimillionaire
26. 'Has money'
27. Wealthy
28. Filthy rich
29. Filthy stinking rich
30. Billionaire
31. 'More money than God'
32. Multibillionaire
33. Mogul
34. Baron
35. Magnate
36. Tycoon
37. Potentate
38. Titan
39. Rockefellow*
40. Trillionaire
41. Quadrillionaire
42. Quintillionaire
43. Sextillionaire
44. Septillionaire
45. Octillionaire
46. Nonillionaire
47. Decillionaire
48. And so on, and so forth ...
49. More money than God

II. Economic Institutions

1. Car boot stall
2. Vendor
3. Shoppe
4. Shop
5. Establishment
6. Company
7. Chain
8. Corporation
9. Multinational corporation
10. Conglomerate
11. Trust
12. Monopoly
13. Command economy

More money than God
1.49

III. Jeans by Price

1. Supermarket/department store own-brand
2. Wrangler
3. Lee
4. Gap
5. Levi's
6. Lucky Brand
7. Firetrap
8. Diesel
9. 7 For All Mankind
10. Citizens of Humanity
11. Sass & Bide
12. Serfontaine
13. G-Star
14. Miss Sixty 'Eden'
15. True Religion
16. Rock & Republic
17. Dolce & Gabbana
18. Antik
19. Adriano Goldschmied

IV. Department Store by Price

1. Oxfam/Salvation Army
2. Out of the wardrobe
3. Primark
4. Argos
5. BHS
6. Debenhams
7. Marks & Spencer
8. Next
9. House of Fraser
10. John Lewis
11. Harvey Nichols
12. Selfridges
13. Fortnum & Mason's
14. Harrods

V. Shirts by Coverage

1. He-Man armour
2. Midriff-exposing cutoff
3. Muscle shirt
4. Wife beater
5. Tank top
6. Sleeveless tank
7. T-shirt
8. Football shirt
9. Long-sleeve shirt
10. Turtleneck
11. Jumper
12. Blazer
13. Jacket
14. Coat
15. Overcoat
16. Parka

VI. Hotel Room Prefixes

1. Presidential
2. Imperial
3. Penthouse
4. Celebrity
5. Ambassador
6. Executive
7. Grand
8. Select
9. European
10. Deluxe
11. Standard

Econo

VI.II

VII. Degrees of Prurient Periodical

1. *Zoo*
2. *Nuts*
3. *FHM*
4. *Maxim*
5. *National Geographic*
6. *Playboy*
7. *Penthouse*
8. *Hustler*
9. Fetish-specific

VIII. Jewellery Merchants by Price

1. Elizabeth Shaw
2. H. Samuel
3. Goldmsmiths
4. Tiffany & Co.
5. Asprey
6. Bvlgari
7. Graff
8. Cartier
9. De Beers
10. Harry Winston

IX. Female House Staff

1. Scullery maids
2. Kitchen maids/between maid/hall girl
3. Nursery maid
4. Chambermaids/ housemaids
5. House parlourmaids/ housemaid
6. Head house parlourmaid/ head housemaid
7. Major doma*
8. Major domus
9. Chief usher (head of White House house staff)
10. Colonel Domus*
11. General Domus*
12. Marshal Domus*
13. Pershing Domus*
14. Supreme Domus*

X. Male House Staff

1. Hall boy
2. Useful man
3. Footman
4. First footman
5. Butler
6. Major domo
7. Major domus
8. Chief usher (head of White House house staff)
9. Colonel Domus*
10. General Domus*
11. Marshal Domus*
12. Pershing Domus*
13. Supreme Domus*

Useful man
X.2

WHAT WE BUILD

I. Degrees of Barrier

1. Shadow
2. Line in the sand
3. Caution tape
4. Danger tape
5. Picket fence
6. Barbed wire
7. Fence
8. Wall
9. Border fence
10. Border wall*
11. Great Wall
12. Breakwater
13. Cofferdam
14. Dam
15. Isthmus
16. Mountain range
17. Earth's gravity
18. Death
19. Ginnungagap*

II. Degrees of Conpull*

1. Thread
2. String
3. Twine
4. Rope
5. Battleship dock-tie rope
6. Cable
7. Chain
8. Anchor chain
9. Bridge cable
10. Space elevator
11. Moon anchor*

III. Degrees of Office Paper Data Storage

1. Post-it note
2. 3x5 card
3. Notepad
4. Legal pad
5. Folder
6. Spiral notebook
7. 3-ring binder
8. Compendium
9. Tome
10. Shelf
11. Wall
12. Library
13. University library
14. University library system
15. The totality of writ

IV. DEGREES OF HOUSE

1. Dollhouse
2. Doghouse
3. Lean-to
4. Outhouse
5. Tent
6. Gazebo
7. Shack
8. Hut
9. Casita
10. Guesthouse
11. House
12. Manse
13. Villa
14. Great house
15. Manor
16. Mansion
17. Hall
18. Estate
19. Castle
20. Chateau
21. Palace
22. Carat*
23. Ingot*
24. Bullion*
25. Vault*
26. Reserve*
27. Home

V. CLASSICAL ARCHITECTURAL PROWESS

1. Brick
2. Post
3. Column
4. Wall
5. Arch
6. Pediment
7. Vault
8. Monument
9. Dome
10. Shrine
11. Temple
12. Church
13. Rotunda
14. Cathedral
15. Palace
16. Basilica
17. Pyramid
18. Wonder
19. Carcallica*
20. Axis mundi
21. Axis soli*
22. Axis galacti*
23. Axis universi*
24. Axis brani*
25. Axis bulki*
26. Axis real*

VI. URBAN GROWTH: CITY SIZES

1. Camp
2. Hamlet
3. Compound
4. Base
5. Village
6. Campus
7. Town
8. Skyscraper
9. Complex
10. City
11. Conurbation
12. Metropolitan area
13. Metropolis
14. Megalopolis
15. Gigalopolis*
16. Teralopolis*
17. Glaciopolis*
18. Enormopolis*
19. Humongopolis*
20. Tremendopolis*
21. Gargantopolis*
22. Behemopolis*
23. Levianopolis*
24. Continopolis*
25. Pancontopolis
26. Pangeopolis*
27. Geopolis*
28. Ecumenopolis**
29. Kardashev 1 civilization**
30. Plurageopolis*
31. Multigeopolis*
32. Solapolis*
33. Pansolapolis*
34. Kardashev 2 civilization**
35. Plurasolapolis*
36. Multisolapolis*
37. Kilosolapolis*
38. Megasolapolis*
39. Gigasolapolis*
40. Galactopolis*
41. Pangalactopolis*
42. Kardashev 3 civilization**
43. Pluragalactopolis*
44. Multigalactopolis*
45. Kilogalactopolis*
46. Gigagalactopolis*
47. Teragalactopolis*
48. Univerpolis*
49. Kardashev 4 civilization**
50. Panuniverpolis*
51. Branopolis*
52. Kardashev 5 civilization**
53. Plurabranopolis*
54. Multibranopolis*
55. Kilobranopolis*
56. Megabranopolis*
57. Megagalactopolis*
58. Gigabranopolis*
59. Terabranopolis*
60. Bulkopolis*
61. Kardashev 6 civilization**
62. The City of God

VII. ROADS BY SIZE

1. Game trail
2. Trail
3. Dirt road
4. Lane
5. Street
6. Road
7. Avenue
8. Boulevard
9. 'A' Road
10. Dual carriageway
11. Motorway
12. Artery
13. Superfreeway*
14. Aorta*
15. Superartery*
16. Branch*
17. Superaorta*
18. Superbranch*
19. Trunk*
20. Supertrunk*

VIII. LIST OF LISTS

1. To-do list
2. Shopping list
3. Batting order
4. Honey-do list
5. Christmas list
6. Family tree
7. This book
8. Phone book
9. Santa's list
10. Census
11. St. Peter's ledger

IX. MAZE DIFFICULTY

1. Alley
2. Corner
3. Topiary maze
4. Caerdroia
5. Troy Town
6. Maze
7. Labyrinth
8. Sigil
9. Escher nightmare*
10. Jareth*
11. Gordion hallway*
12. Dwinelle*

MILITARY RANKS

I. Degrees of Fortification

1. Concealment
2. Cover
3. Cover and concealment
4. Foxhole
5. Trench
6. Bunker
7. Māori pā
8. Wagon circle
9. Wall
10. Tower
11. Fort
12. Keep
13. Castle
14. Fortress
15. Citadel
16. Great wall
17. Ring fortress
18. Maginot*
19. Norad*
20. Strategic Defense Initiative*
21. Meteor Defense Complex*
22. Planetary Intent Defense*
23. Ragnoridel*
24. Hard planet*
25. Hard star*
26. Hard galaxy*

Soldier

IV. I

II. CHAIN OF COMMAND

1. Private
2. Corporal
3. Sergeant
4. Lieutenant
5. Captain
6. Major
7. Colonel
8. Brigadier
9. General
10. Field Marshal
11. Pershing*

III. EQUIVALENT MILITARY RANK: FOUR-STAR GENERAL AND ABOVE

1. Four-star: General, admiral, marshal
2. Five-star: General of the Army, Fleet Admiral, Grand Admiral, Field Marshal, Mushir
3. Six-star: General of the Armies, Admiral of the Navy, Wonsu, Generalissimo, reichsmarschall, First Marshal of the Empire, Marshal of the Soviet Union, Admiral of the Fleet of the Soviet Union
4. Supreme military authority: Commander-in-chief, shogun, magister militum, chairman of the Central Military Commission

IV. MILITARY UNITS ON LAND

1. Soldier
2. Fire team
3. Squad
4. Platoon
5. Company
6. Battalion
7. Regiment
8. Brigade
9. Legion
10. Division
11. Corps
12. Army
13. Army group/La Grand Armée
14. Pershing*
15. Land force
16. Navada*
17. Armag*
18. Ragnad*
19. Behemotag*

V. MILITARY UNITS IN AIR

1. Aircraft
2. Section
3. Flight
4. Squadron
5. Wing
6. Group
7. Numbered air force
8. Air command
9. Air force
10. Airmada*
11. Airmag*
12. Ziztag*

Cutter

VI.1

VI. Military Units on Water or in Space

1. Cutter
2. Corvette
3. Destroyer
4. Frigate
5. Cruiser
6. Dreadnought
7. Heavy cruiser
8. Battlecruiser
9. Battleship
10. Carrier
11. Capital ship
12. Squadron
13. Carrier group
14. Flotilla
15. Battle group
16. Fleet
17. Armada
18. Helen*
19. Leviatag*

VII. Caliber Calliper

1. Spitball
2. Nerf arrow
3. BB gun
4. Air pistol/rifle
5. Arrow
6. .22
7. Pistol
8. Rifle
9. .357 Magnum
10. .50 cal
11. Shotgun
12. Mortar
13. Culverin
14. Cannon
15. Artillery
16. Howitzer
17. Battleship main gun
18. Big Bertha
19. Paris Gun
20. Supercannon
21. The Death Star's tributary turbolaser

VIII. COMBAT

1. Tiff
2. Spat
3. Altercation
4. Bitch slap
5. Scuffle
6. Fight
7. Punch-up
8. Donnybrook
9. Free-for-all
10. Brawl
11. Rumble
12. Skirmish
13. Clash
14. Feud
15. Engagement
16. Raid
17. Attack
18. Assault
19. Charge
20. Melee
21. Battle
22. Strategic withdrawal
23. Offensive
24. Blitzkrieg
25. Revolution
26. Campaign
27. Conquest
28. Civil war
29. War
30. Crusade/jihad
31. War of attrition
32. World war
33. Limited nuclear exchange
34. Full nuclear exchange
35. Armageddon
36. Ragnarok*
37. Titanomachy/gigantomachy
38. Multigeddon*
39. Tectonomachy*
40. Plurageddon*
41. Pangeddon*
42. Galactogeddon*
43. Pangalactogeddon*
44. Pluragalactogeddon*
45. Multigalactogeddon*
46. Univegeddon*
47. Panunivegeddon*
48. Pluraunivegeddon*
49. Multiunivegeddon*
50. Bulkogeddon*
51. Omnigeddon*

IX. WATER GUNS

1. Cupped hands
2. Thumb over tap
3. Water pistol
4. Super soaker

5. Garden hose
6. Fire hose
7. Fire Monitor

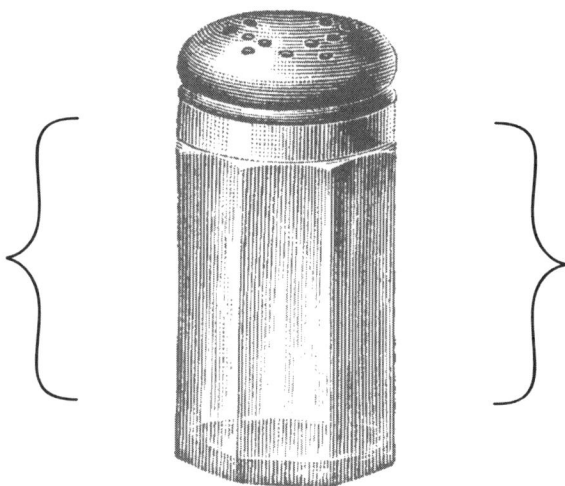

Assault

VIII.18

THE POLITICAL ARENA

I. Pundit Hyperbole: Frankly, the Actions of _____ Are …

1. Godlike
2. A perfect sphere of golden light
3. Infallible
4. Inspiring
5. Solomonic
6. Great
7. Wonderful
8. Beyond reproach
9. Mostly right
10. Well-intentioned/ well-meaning
11. Not perfect, but …
12. Within reproach
13. Ineffectual
14. Short-sighted
15. Foolhardy
16. Mistaken
17. Wrong
18. Ridiculous
19. Preposterous
20. Offensive
21. Detestable
22. Shameful
23. Outrageous
24. Contemptible
25. Malevolent
26. Beneath contempt
27. Beyond contempt
28. Beyond the pale
29. Barbaric
30. Evil
31. Not worthy of being dignified with a response
32. Vile
33. Unthinkable
34. Worse than Hitler

Preposterous
I.19

II. THE POLITICAL SPECTRUM

1. Communist
2. Marxist
3. Socialist
4. Green Party
5. Labour
6. Liberal Democrat
7. Conservative
8. UKIP
9. BNP
10. Anarchist
11. Raving Loony Party

III. RULE OF LAW

1. Subtext
2. Polite suggestion
3. Decorum/etiquette/ local custom
4. Rule
5. Precept
6. Bylaw
7. Executive order
8. Law
9. Constitutional amendment
10. Constitutional article
11. Unchangeable constitutional element
12. Natural law
13. Physical law

IV. TOP RANKS OF THE OLD WORLD

1. Royal: khan, sultan, king
2. Imperial: great khan, caliph, emperor
3. Patriarch: Dalai Lama, imam, Pope
4. Nexus protagonist*: Siddhartha Gautama, Muhammad, Jesus Christ
5. Supreme divinity: Brahman, Allah, YHWH

V. Ultimate Power: Absolute Secular Authority

1. Clan chief
2. Village headman
3. Headman
4. Chief
5. Chieftain
6. High chief
7. Paramount chief
8. King
9. Emperor
10. Paramount*

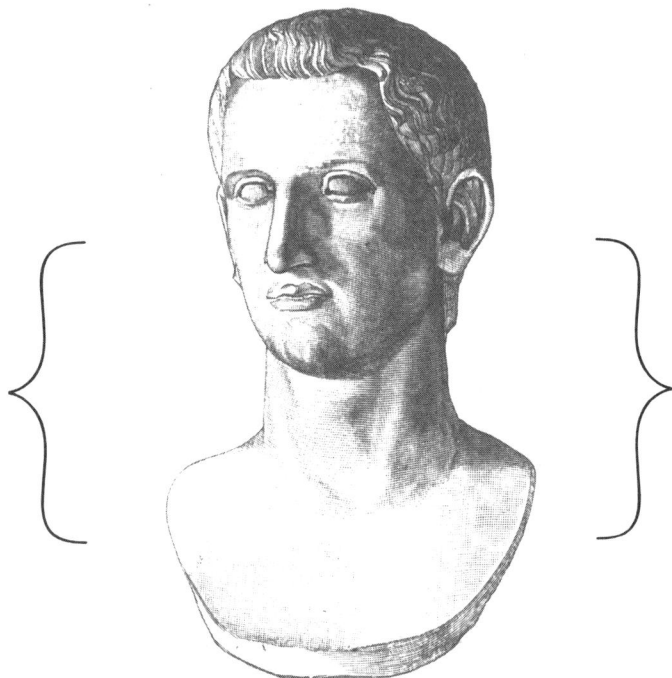

Emperor
v.9

VI. Foreign Relations

1. Unitary state
2. Regional state
3. Federal state
4. Confederation
5. Treaty organization/ Alliance
6. International organization
7. Diplomatic relations with
8. Neutral
9. No diplomatic relations with
10. Sanctions
11. Embargo
12. Blockade
13. Border skirmish
14. Air assault
15. Undeclared war
16. Declared war
17. Total war
18. Limited nuclear war/ regional nuclear war
19. Absolute war
20. Mutual attempted extermination/war to the last man, woman, and child/war of extinction/rancomachy*

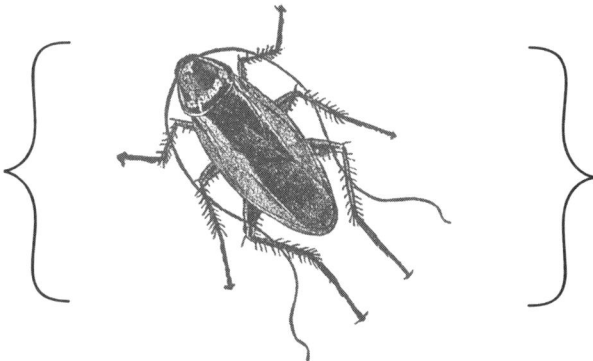

*Rancomachy**
VI.20

1. Partnership
2. Family
3. Clan
4. Village
5. Estate
6. Tribe
7. Cult
8. Township
9. City
10. Barony
11. City-state
12. Viscounty
13. County/parish
14. Duchy/emirate
15. Principality
16. Grand Duchy
17. Lordship
18. Territory
19. Province
20. State
21. Kingdom/sultanate/khanate
22. Nation
23. Empire/caliphate/great khanate
24. Plateau*
25. Superpower
26. Hyperpower
27. Archpire*
28. Panpire*
29. Terrapire*
30. Ecumenopire*
31. Kardashev 1 civilization*
32. Plurageopire*
33. Multigeopire*
34. Dyson swarm**
35. Solapire*
36. Pansolapire*
37. Kardashev 2 civilization*/Dyson sphere**
38. Plurasolapire*
39. Multisolapire*
40. Kilosolapire*
41. Megasolapire*
42. Gigasolopire*
43. Galactopire*
44. Pangalactopire*
45. Kardashev 3 civilization*
46. Pluragalactopire*
47. Multigalactopire*
48. Kilogalactopire*
49. Megagalactopire*
50. Gigagalactopire*
51. Teragalactopire*
52. Univerpire*
53. Kardashev 4 civilization*/Panuniverpire*
54. Kardashev 5 civilization*/Branopire*
55. Panbranopire*
56. Plurabranopire*
57. Multibranopire*
58. Kilobranopire*
59. Megabranopire*
60. Gigabranopire*
61. Terabranopire*

VIII. Contractual Agreements

1. Assumption
2. Indication
3. Understanding
4. Assurance
5. Agreement
6. Promise
7. Handshake
8. Deal
9. Guarantee
10. Bond
11. Swear
12. Pinky swear
13. Guarantee
14. Pledge
15. Ironclad guarantee
16. Gentlemen's agreement
17. Oral contract
18. Written contract
19. Oath
20. Writ
21. Pact
22. Compact
23. Treaty
24. Concordat
25. Covenant
26. Divinant*
27. Uttol*

Bond

VIII.10

THE NATURAL WORLD

I. Darwinian Prowess

1. Annulled
2. Lost
3. Fossilized without DNA
4. Fossilized with DNA
5. Prehistoric
6. Extinct
7. Extinct in the wild
8. Critical
9. Endangered
10. Vulnerable
11. Lower risk
12. Secure
13. The Winner*

II. The Speed of Multipedal Locomotion

1. Standing still
2. Inch
3. Sniper low crawl
4. Grovel
5. Wriggle
6. Creep
7. Low crawl
8. Crawl
9. Slither
10. Scuff
11. Shuffle
12. Hands-and-knees crawl
13. Limp
14. Shamble
15. Slog
16. Trudge
17. Plod
18. Pad
19. Draggle
20. Lumber
21. Stump
22. Toddle
23. Mosey
24. Straggle
25. Trek
26. Saunter
27. Amble
28. Stroll
29. Sashay
30. Promenade
31. Ramble
32. Walk
33. Stalk
34. Traipse
35. Hoof it/leg it/foot it
36. March
37. Tramp
38. Hike
39. Pace/rack
40. Quick time
41. Stride
42. Power walk
43. Skip
44. Trot
45. Dogtrot
46. Prance
47. Bound

48. Scoot
49. Double time
50. Jog
51. Lope
52. Scamper
53. Scurry
54. Run
55. Canter
56. Skedaddle
57. Hotfoot
58. Race
59. Scud
60. Sprint
61. Tear

62. Dash
63. Dart
64. Hightail
65. Full sprint
66. Flat-out
67. Owen*
68. Gallop
69. Full gallop
70. Band*
71. Burst*
72. Cheet*
73. Blur
74. Flash*

The Winner

1.13

III. QUANTITIES OF WOOD

1. Cell
2. Speck of sawdust
3. Splinter
4. Shaving
5. Splint
6. Whittling
7. Stick
8. Lumber
9. Timber
10. Log
11. Trunk
12. Tree
13. Stand
14. Copse
15. Grove
16. Forest
17. Biome
18. Fuzzy crust/ Fuzzy planet*
19. Red spot knot*

IV. DEGREES OF LIFE

1. Organic molecule
2. Virus
3. Organelles and other subcellular structures
4. Cell
5. Tissue
6. Organ
7. System
8. Organism
9. Ecosystem
10. Biome
11. Biosphere
12. The panspermial anticlasm*

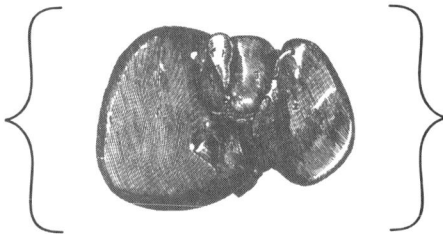

Organ
IV.6

V. DEGREES OF ICE

1. Two water molecules frozen together
2. Snowflake twig
3. Snowflake branch
4. Snowflake
5. Shaving
6. Chip
7. Cube
8. Icicle
9. Snowball
10. Ice block
11. Snowman
12. Snowdrift
13. Frozen lake
14. Comet
15. Iceberg
16. Glacier
17. Ice sheet
18. Ice shelf
19. Ice cap
20. Ice age
21. Snowball Earth/ snowball planet
22. Oortberg*
23. Oort glacier*
24. Oort shelf*
25. Oort cap*
26. Solid oort sphere*
27. Oort cloud
28. Kardashev reservoir*

VI. DEGREES OF WETNESS

1. Dehydrated
2. Lyophilized
3. Bone-dry
4. Arid
5. Parched
6. Dry
7. Damp
8. Moist
9. Wet
10. Dripping
11. Wringing wet
12. Sodden
13. Drenched
14. Waterlogged
15. Sopping
16. Soaked
17. Saturated

VII. BODIES OF WATER

1. Drizzlet*
2. Driplet*
3. Droplet
4. Drop
5. Gleek
6. Squirt
7. Dribble
8. Trickle
9. Ripple
10. Splash
11. Cup
12. Puddle
13. Bucket
14. Wake
15. Barrel
16. Pond
17. Stream
18. Pool
19. Creek
20. Brook
21. Wave
22. River
23. Tidal wave
24. Lake
25. Flood
26. Tsunami
27. Amazile*
28. Inundation
29. Deluge
30. Sea
31. Panamazile*
32. Scabland generator*/ Augscab*/Missoula Flood/Spokane Flood/ Bretz Flood
33. Ocean
34. The Deluge
35. Super-ocean
36. Water planet
37. Saturn ocean/ Joviocean*

VIII. DEGREES OF FISSURE

1. Fracture
2. Crack
3. Fissure
4. Fault
5. Crevasse
6. Gorge
7. Canyon
8. Ocean trench
9. Chasm
10. Planetary isthmus*
11. Event horizon
12. Ginnungagap*

IX. LAND SURROUNDED BY WATER

1. Larson*
2. Islet
3. Island
4. Continent
5. Supercontinent
6. Pangea

X. LAND MASS AND GEOLOGICAL FORMS

1. Anthill
2. Molehill
3. Pile
4. Berm
5. Bluff
6. Knoll
7. Dune
8. Hillock
9. Hill
10. Mesa
11. Mountain
12. Peak
13. Plateau
14. Mountain range
15. Tectonic plate
16. Continent
17. Supercontinent
18. Pangea
19. Crust

The Deluge
VII.34

XI. Sizes of Earth

The list that launched a thousand words

1. Oxtilith*
2. Femtolith*
3. Picolith*
4. Nanolith*
5. Microlith*
6. Smithereen
7. Grain
8. Millilith*
9. Pebble
10. Rock
11. Centilith*
12. Stone
13. Decilith*
14. Slab
15. Boulder
16. Monolith
17. Megalith
18. Meteor
19. Asteroid
20. Gigalith*
21. Tetralith*
22. Moon
23. Planetesimal
24. Pentalith*
25. Dwarf planet
26. Protoplanet
27. Planet
28. Exalith*
29. Zettalith*
30. Yottalith*
31. Galactolith*
32. Oxtalith*
33. Universolith*
34. Branolith*
35. Bulkolith*
36. Omnilith*

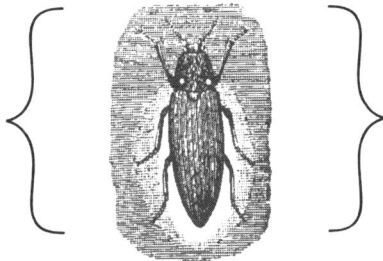

Firefly
XII.5

XII. LEVELS OF BRIGHTNESS: SCIENTIFIC

1. One photon
2. LED
3. Night light
4. Christmas light
5. Firefly
6. Candle
7. Flashlight
8. Flare
9. Standard 100-watt light bulb
10. Dipped headlights
11. Halogen
12. Main beams
13. Magnesium
14. Floodlight
15. Fireworks
16. Albert Speer's 'Cathedral of Light'
17. Nuclear bomb
18. Tunguska
19. Hydrogen bomb
20. Planet killer asteroid (Dottie)
21. Star
22. Galaxy
23. Supernova
24. Gamma-ray burst
25. Quasar
26. The Big Bang

XIII. CANDLEPOWER: DESCRIPTIONS OF BRIGHTNESS

1. Cavern black
2. Pitch black
3. Dark
4. Flickering
5. Glowing
6. Gleaming
7. Luminous
8. Lanternic*
9. Effulgent
10. Bright
11. Refulgent
12. Lambent
13. Brilliant
14. Radiant
15. Hand-lifting*
16. Elbow-lifting*
17. Blinding
18. Superlambent*
19. Nuclear
20. Hyperlambent*
21. Supernova bright
22. GRBic*
23. Augocosmic*

XIV. Temperature by Degrees

1. Negative kelvin
2. Absolute zero
3. Black hole singularity
4. Near zero
5. Liquid nitrogen
6. One-hundred-dog night**
7. Polar
8. Hyperborean
9. Six-dog night**
10. Arctic
11. Five-dog night**
12. Sub-zero
13. Frigid
14. Four-dog night**
15. Gelid
16. Icy
17. Three-dog night**
18. Severe
19. Frore
20. Below freezing
21. Freezing
22. Penetrating cold
23. Two-dog night**
24. Piercing cold
25. Bitter cold
26. Sharp
27. Biting cold
28. Nipping
29. Stinging cold
30. Boreal
31. Wintry
32. One-dog night**
33. Rimy
34. Sleety
35. Nippy
36. Raw
37. Snappy
38. Cold
39. Nipply
40. Brumal/hiemal
41. Cool
42. Parky
43. Brisk
44. Crisp
45. Chilly
46. Room temperature
47. Tepid
48. Lukewarm
49. Warm
50. Calescent
51. Feverish
52. Hot
53. Sweltering
54. Sultry
55. Torrid
56. Piping hot
57. Scalding
58. Blistering
59. Boiling
60. Burning
61. Scorching
62. Decalescent
63. Searing
64. Blazing
65. White hot
66. Surface of the sun
67. Fission
68. Fusion

69. Plasma
70. Core of the sun
71. Immediate vicinity of a black hole singularity
72. Supernova
73. Gamma-ray burst
74. Oh-my-God particle collisions
75. Beginning of the Big Bang/Planck temperature
76. Theory of everything excitations, Landau pole, Extradimensional Gauge Freedom

XV. DEGREES OF OPACITY

1. Lead
2. Opaque
3. Translucent
4. Transparent
5. Vacuum

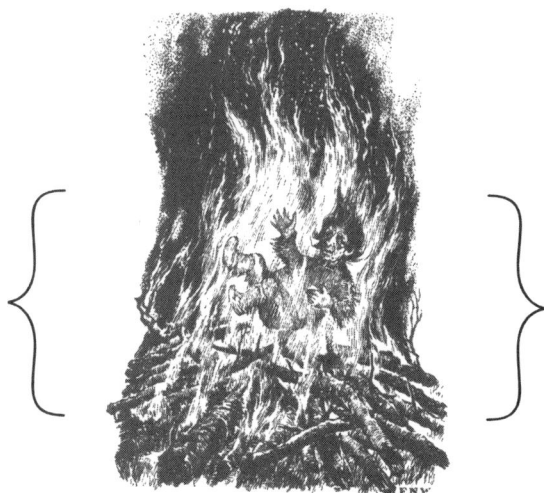

Hot

XIV.52

XVI. OBJECT SIZES

1. Infinitesimal
2. String scale
3. Nano scale
4. Sub-atomic scale
5. Atomic
6. Molecular
7. Mitochondriatic
8. Cellular
9. Microscopic
10. Smaller than the eye can see
11. Miniscule
12. Elfin
13. Tiny
14. Lilliputian
15. Small
16. Medium
17. Bulky
18. Large
19. Big
20. Jumbo
21. Immense
22. Massive
23. Hulking
24. Whopping
25. Walloping
26. Giant
27. Mammoth
28. Huge
29. Rorqualic*
30. Enormous
31. Colossal
32. Tremendous
33. Zizic*
34. Gigantic
35. Brobdingnagian
36. Humongous
37. Gargantuan
38. Leviathan
39. Stupendous
40. Mountainous
41. Titanic
42. Vast
43. Behemoth
44. Pangeic*
45. Terrestrial*
46. Jovian*
47. Astronomic
48. Star cluster scale
49. Galactic
50. Galaxy group scale
51. Galaxy cluster scale
52. Super-cluster scale
53. Walls-and-voids scale
54. Super-gravitational scale
55. Cosmic
56. Universal
57. Macrodimensional*
58. Interdimensional*
59. Omnidimensional*
60. Bulkous*

XVII. VALUE OF MASS

1. Aggregate
2. Dirt
3. Sand
4. Oil
5. Coal
6. Water
7. Wood
8. Plastic
9. Aluminium
10. Steel
11. Stainless steel
12. Bronze
13. Silver
14. Gold
15. Platinum
16. Ruby
17. Diamond
18. Plutonium
19. Red Diamond
20. Californium

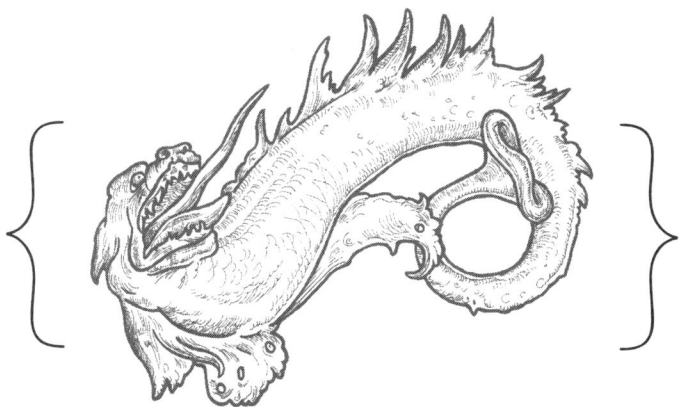

Leviathan
XVI.38

XVIII. SEGMENTS OF TIME

1. No time
2. Absolute increment*
3. Planck time
4. Planck epoch
5. Grand unification epoch
6. Nanosecond
7. Electroweak epoch
8. Truti
9. Hadron epoch
10. Microsecond
11. Renu
12. Millisecond
13. Lava
14. Leekshaka
15. Second
16. Moment
17. Paramanu (average blink interval)
18. 'No time'
19. Real quick
20. Vighati
21. New York minute
22. Minute
23. Post-haste
24. Lepton epoch
25. Alto
26. Ghati
27. Little bit
28. Muhurta
29. Hour
30. While
31. Day
32. Nakshatra ahoratram
33. Weekend
34. Workweek
35. Week
36. Fortnight
37. Tithi
38. Lunar month/lunar cycle/Masa
39. Month
40. A dog year
41. Ruthu
42. Season
43. Aayana
44. A month of Sundays
45. Year
46. Leap year/ intercalary year
47. Blue moon
48. Donkey's years
49. Decade
50. Coon's age
51. Dog's age
52. Metonic cycle
53. Generation
54. Callipic Cycle
55. Lifetime
56. Century
57. Historic period
58. Millennium
59. Historic age
60. Historic era*
61. Historic eon*
62. Epoch of nucleosynthesis
63. Geologic stage
64. Geologic epoch
65. Megannum
66. Geologic period/system
67. Mahayuga

68. Geologic era
69. Astronomic age
70. Manvantara
71. Geologic eon
72. Gigannum
73. Starlife*
74. Kalpa
75. Day and Night of Brahma
76. Astronomic era
77. Astronomic eon
78. Branelife*
79. Tetrannum

80. Year of Brahma
81. Life Cycle of Brahma
82. Pentannum*
83. Exannum*
84. Zettannum*
85. Yottannum*
86. Oxtannum*
87. Bulklife
88. Until the end of time
89. Chronotangential*
90. Eternity

Hour

XVIII.29

XIX. The Rate of Speed

1. Relativistically still
2. Still
3. Snail's pace
4. Sloth's pace
5. Slow as molasses
6. Slow
7. Brisk
8. Quick
9. Rapid
10. Bicycling speed
11. Fast
12. Driving
13. Breakneck speed
14. Fast as a bat out of hell
15. Airliner-cruising-altitude speed
16. The speed of sound
17. Supersonic
18. Speeding bullet
19. Escape velocity
20. Lorentzian speed
21. Light speed/the speed of gravity
22. Superluminal
23. Ridiculous speed
24. Ludicrous speed, a.k.a. Going Plaid (from *Spaceballs*)
25. God speed*

Snail's pace
XIX.3

XX. THE DISTANCE BETWEEN TWO POINTS

Zeno was wrong.

1. A point
2. Infinitesimeter (a.k.a. Zenometer)*
3. Overgoogolplexometer*
4. Overgoogolmeter*
5. Oxtimeter*
6. Yoctometer
7. Zeptometer
8. Attometer
9. Femtometer
10. Picometer
11. Bohr radius
12. Ångström
13. Nanometer
14. Micrometer
15. Millimeter
16. Centimeter
17. Inch
18. Hand
19. Decimeter
20. Foot
21. Hop
22. Cubit
23. Skip
24. Jump
25. Yard
26. Meter
27. Pole
28. Hop, skip, and a jump
29. Decameter
30. Chain
31. Hectometer
32. Furlong
33. Kilometer
34. Russian verst
35. Roman mile
36. Statute mile
37. International mile
38. U.S. survey mile
39. Scotch mile
40. Nautical mile
41. Geographical mile
42. Irish mile
43. Parasang
44. League
45. Ole Romer mile
46. Austrian meile
47. Ways
48. Marathon
49. Megameter
50. Gigameter
51. Tetameter
52. Parsec
53. Pentameter
54. Light-year
55. Exameter
56. Zettameter
57. Kiloparsec
58. Yottameter
59. Megaparsec
60. Oxtameter
61. Gigaparsec
62. Total radius
63. Total diameter
64. Total circumference

65. Tetraparsec
66. Pentaparsec
67. Exaparsec
68. Zettaparsec
69. Yottaparsec
70. Oxtaparsec*
71. Googolmeter*
72. Googolparsec*
73. Googolplexmeter*
74. Googolplexparsec*
75. Length of the theoretical eleventh dimension
76. Infinimeter, infiniparsec, infiniångström, etc.*

XXI. DEGREES OF HARDNESS

1. Formless
2. Fluid
3. Slushy
4. Mushy
5. Squishy
6. Soft
7. Gelatinous
8. Spongy
9. Flimsy
10. Moldable
11. Elastic
12. Limp
13. Malleable
14. Yielding
15. Firm
16. Inflexible
17. Stiff
18. Indurate
19. Hard
20. Solid
21. Rock-hard
22. Ferrous
23. Rigid
24. Diamond
25. Adamant

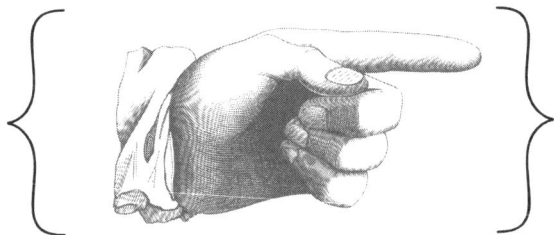

A point
XX.1

XXII. Non-Numerical Elastic Quantities

1. None, zero, nothing, void, scratch, nil, nada, nullity, nix, nought, naught
2. A
3. One and change
4. A couple
5. Hardly any
6. A few
7. Some
8. Several
9. A deal
10. A grip
11. A cluster
12. Umpteen
13. A batch
14. Gobs
15. A flock
16. A hatful
17. A mess
18. Plenty
19. Numerous
20. Many
21. Quite a little
22. A good deal
23. A mickle
24. Quite a few
25. A lot
26. A tidy sum
27. A whole lot
28. Quite a lot
29. Lots
30. A peck
31. A passel
32. A stack
33. Plenty
34. A mass
35. A muckle
36. A spate
37. A wad
38. A great deal
39. Scads
40. A half-slew*
41. A raft
42. A pile
43. Oodles
44. Crawling with
45. Piles
46. Rafts
47. Heaps
48. Multitudes
49. Rife with
50. Slew/a whole slew
51. Large numbers of
52. Swarming with
53. Tons
54. Lousy with
55. Abundant
56. Bountiful/bounteous
57. Profuse
58. Copious
59. A sight of
60. Teeming with
61. Abounding
62. Legion
63. Horde
64. Untold
65. A mint
66. More than you can shake a stick at
67. Far as the eye can see

68. Dizzying
69. Myriad
70. Uncounted
71. Measureless
72. Inconceivable amount
73. Jillion
74. Zillion
75. Kajillion
76. Kazillion

77. Uncountable
78. Immeasurable
79. Innumerable
80. Incalculable
81. Unballparkable*
82. Numberless/countless
83. Boundless
84. Limitless
85. Endless

A flock
XXII.15

THESAURUS OF EXTREMES

1. Aught, cipher, cypher, nil, none, nought, null, ought, oh, zilch, squat (0)
2. Fine-structure constant/ Sommerfeld fine structure constant ($1/137.0359997...$)
3. Karat ($5/120$ OR 0.04166 ...)
4. Copeland-Erdós constant (0.2357111317192329 ...)
5. Quarter ($1/4$ OR 0.25)
6. Meissel-Mertens constant (0.26149721 ...)
7. Bernstein's constant (0.28016949 ...)
8. Gauss-Kuzmin-Wirsing constant (0.3036630029 ...)
9. Hafner-Sarnak-McCurley constant (0.35323637 ...)
10. Prouhet-Thue-Morse constant (0.4124503364 ...)
11. Prime constant (0.414682509851 ...)
12. Half ($1/2$ OR 0.5)
13. Landau constant ($1/2 < L < 0.544$)
14. Omega constant (0.56714 ...)
15. Euler-Mascheroni constant (0.577215664 ...)
16. Twin primes constant (0.66016181 ...)
17. Golomb-Dickman constant (0.62432998 ...)
18. Cahen's constant (0.6434105462 ...)
19. Laplace limit (0.66274341 ...)
20. Embree-Trefethen constant (0.70258 ...)
21. Landau-Ramanujan constant (0.764223653 ...)
22. Alladi-Grinstead constant (0.80939402 ...)
23. Gauss's constant (0.8346268 ...)
24. Brun's constant for prime quadruplets (0.87058838 ...)
25. Catalan's constant (0.915965594177 ...)
26. A/single/ace, singleton, unary, unit (1)
27. Legendre's constant (1.08366 ...)
28. Lengyel's constant (1.0986858 ...)
29. Viswanath's constant (1.13198824 ...)
30. Khinchin-Lévy constant (1.1865691 ...)
31. Apéry's constant (1.2020569 ...)
32. Mills' constant (1.30637788 ...)
33. Plastic number/ silver number (1.324718 ...)

34. Pythagoras's constant/square root of 2 (1.414213562 ...)
35. Ramanujan-Soldner constant (1.45136923 ...)
36. Backhouse's constant (1.456074948582 ...)
37. Porter's constant (1.46707807 ...)
38. Erdós-Borwein constant (1.60669515 ...)
39. Golden ratio/phi (1.61803398 ...)
40. Niven's constant (1.705211 ...)
41. Theodorus's constant/square root of 3 (1.732050807 ...)
42. Brun's constant for twin primes (1.9021605 ...)
43. Pair/brace/couple/ dual/duo/dyad/twain twin/twosome/yoke (2)
44. Silver ratio (2.41421356 ...)
45. Second Feigenbaum constant (2.50290787 ...)
46. Sierpiski's constant (2.584981759 ...)
47. Gelfond-Schneider constant (2.6651441 ...)
48. Khinchin's constant (2.685452001 ...)
49. e/Euler's number/ Napier's constant (2.7182818284 ...)
50. Fransén-Robinson constant (2.80777024 ...)
51. Trio/triumvirate/ leash/ternion/triplet/ trey/ (3)
52. Pi/Archimedes' constant/Ludolph's number (3.141592653589793 ...)
53. Quartet/tetrad (4)
54. First Feigenbaum constant (4.669201609 ...)
55. Quint/quintet/ pentad/a basketball team (5)
56. Half a dozen (6)
57. Heptad/seplet/ septuplet (7)
58. Octad/octet/otonary/ octuplet/ogdoad (8)
59. Ennead (9)
60. Decade (10)
61. Dozen (12)
62. Baker's dozen/long dozen (13)
63. Score/Indian (20)
64. Case/quire (24)
65. Sorok (40)
66. Shock (60)
67. Century/short hundred/ centred/ton (100)
68. Gross hundred/long hundred/great hundred (120)

69. Gross/great dozen (144)
70. Old ream (480)
71. Ream (500)
72. Printer's ream/perfect ream (516)
73. Grand/bundle/chiliad/ yard/K (1,000)
74. Great gross/long gross/ dozen gross (1,728)
75. Ton (2,000)
76. Printer's case (4,000)
77. Bale (5,000)
78. Myriad (10,000)
79. Lakh (100,000)
80. Crore (10,000,000)
81. Mole (6.022×10^{23})
82. Googol (10^{100})
83. Great mole (A MOLE MOLES)
84. Googolplex (10^{GOOGOL})

Maul
XXIV.17

XXIV. Degrees of Destruction

1. Tap
2. Squeeze
3. Disturb
4. Squoosh
5. Scratch
6. Squish
7. Slam
8. Wallop
9. Beat
10. Scrunch
11. Vitiate
12. Clobber
13. Wreck
14. Break
15. Smite
16. Smash
17. Maul
18. Slay
19. Total
20. Demolish
21. Crush
22. Abate
23. Decimate
24. Terminate
25. Pulverize
26. Destroy
27. Shatter
28. Frappé
29. Obliterate
30. Annihilate
31. Dissolve
32. Vaporize
33. De-atomize
34. Disintegrate
35. Convert to energy
36. Change to Hawking radiation with infomation preserved
37. Change to Hawking radiation without information preserved
38. Erase
39. Annul

XXV. Parts of a Whole

1. None/squat
2. Quantum
3. Atom
4. Molecule
5. Particle
6. Diddly-squat
7. Whiff
8. Iota
9. Trace
10. Soupçon
11. Tittle
12. Speck
13. Scintilla
14. Jot
15. Diddly
16. Smithereen
17. Crumb
18. Smidgen

19. Chip
20. Negligible
21. Shred
22. Dram
23. Scrap
24. Bit
25. Modicum
26. Touch
27. Chicken feed
28. Spot
29. Two-bit
30. Tiny fraction
31. Morsel
32. A little
33. Some
34. Quarter
35. Chunk
36. Major part
37. Hunk
38. Plurality
39. Half/even-steven
40. Most/majority
41. Big half
42. The better part
43. The meat
44. The lion's share
45. A two-thirds majority
46. Overwhelming majority
47. Preponderance
48. The body
49. The bulk
50. Vast majority
51. The whole

XXVI. Comparison in Pairs

1. The same
2. Selfsame
3. Identical
4. Clone
5. Duplicate
6. Double
7. Facsimile
8. Copy
9. Indistinguishable
10. Xerox
11. Twin
12. Symmetrical
13. Parallel
14. Equal
15. Synonymic
16. Coincident
17. Interchangeable
18. Analogous
19. Basically the same
20. Dead ringer
21. Spitting image
22. Matching
23. Lookalike
24. Dopplegänger
25. Conterminous
26. Congruent
27. Cognate
28. Asymmetrical
29. Alike
30. Similar
31. Unequal
32. Uneven

33. Comparable
34. Different
35. Distinct
36. Dissimilar
37. Unalike
38. Divergent
39. Contrasting
40. A far cry
41. Unique
42. Unassociated
43. Contrary
44. Opposed
45. Incommensurable
46. Contradistinctive
47. Conflicting
48. Opposite
49. Diametric
50. Antithetical
51. Disparate
52. Polar opposite
53. Diametrically opposed
54. Antipodal
55. Contrapositive
56. Incomparable

Clone

XXVI.4

XXVII. Comparison in Groups of Three or More

1. Selfsame
2. Identical/Identic
3. Equivalent
4. Clone
5. Duplicated
6. Tantamount
7. Facsimile
8. Copied
9. Indistinguishable
10. Homomorphic
11. Borgic*
12. Parallel
13. Homologous
14. Uniform
15. Conforming
16. Institutionalized
17. Matching
18. Systematized
19. Undifferentiated
20. Normalized
21. Commensurate
22. Consubstantial
23. Agnate
24. Consistent
25. Congruous
26. Homogenized
27. Homogeneous
28. Akin
29. Alike
30. Consanguine
31. Similar
32. Distinctive
33. Dissimilar
34. Varied
35. Differing
36. Discrepant
37. Mixed
38. Sundry
39. Assorted
40. Various
41. Hodgepodge
42. Salmagundi
43. Potpourri
44. A mixed bag
45. Differentiated
46. Diverse
47. Motley
48. Variform
49. Heterogeneous
50. Heterogenized
51. Variegated
52. Diversified
53. Manifold
54. Diversiform
55. Multifarious
56. Miscellaneous
57. Wide-ranging
58. Unrelated
59. Discrepant
60. Clashing
61. Jarring
62. Contradistinctive
63. Disparate
64. Incommensurate
65. Antipotive*
66. Omniform
67. Omnifarious
68. Omnigeneous*
69. Omnique*

XXVIII. Taxonomic Elements

1. Living thing
2. Family unit
3. Clan
4. Tribe
5. Ethnicity
6. Race
7. Subspecies
8. Species
9. Subgenus
10. Genus
11. Infrafamily
12. Subfamily
13. Family
14. Superfamily
15. Infraorder
16. Suborder
17. Order
18. Subclass
19. Class
20. Subphylum/ subdivision
21. Phylum/division
22. Kingdom
23. Domain
24. Empire
25. Biota/vitae
    LIFE SCIENCE V. OTHER PHYSICAL SCIENCE
26. Panpire a.k.a. plateau*
    EMPIRICAL SCIENCE V. MATHEMATICAL SCIENCE*
27. Terrapire*
    PURE SCIENCE V. APPLIED SCIENCE
28. Solapire*
    SCIENCE V. OTHER ACADEMICS
29. Galactopire*
    ACADEMICS V. INFORMAL KNOWLEDGE
30. Branopire*
    THAT WHICH IS KNOWN V. THAT WHICH IS UNKNOWN
31. Bulkpire*
    THAT WHICH IS REAL V. THAT WHICH IS NOT REAL

XXIX. Times Through the Ages

1. Before time began
2. In the beginning ...
3. Primordial
4. Primeval
5. Prehistoric
6. Ancient
7. Medieval
8. Recent
9. Modern
10. In a bit
11. In a while
12. Tomorrow
13. Whenever
14. Soon
15. Eventually
16. The near future
17. The future
18. In my lifetime
19. The distant future
20. Until the end of time
21. Never

1. Nothing
2. Chaos
3. Random
4. Omnientropic*
5. Omniclysmic*
6. Cacomorphic*
7. Chaotic
8. Maelstrom
9. Pandemonium
10. Bedlam
11. Anarchic
12. Turvy*
13. Tumultuous
14. Havoc
15. Mare's nest
16. Helter*
17. Haphazard
18. Helter skelter
19. Turbulent
20. Can of worms
21. Snarled
22. Tangled
23. Rat's nest
24. Pigpen
25. Shambles
26. Disheveled
27. Mixed-up
28. Topsy-turvy
29. Confused
30. Pell-mell
31. Cluttered
32. Jumbled
33. Mussy
34. Littered
35. Messy
36. Un-neat
37. Sloppy
38. Tousled
39. Disordered/ unorderly
40. Untidy
41. Disarrayed
42. Disorganized
43. Muddled
44. Unstructured
45. Disjointed
46. Cockeyed
47. Bedraggled
48. Disarranged
49. Uncluttered
50. Unsystematic
51. Arrayed
52. Neat
53. Tidy
54. Trim
55. Orderly
56. Arranged
57. Serial
58. Regular
59. Patterned
60. Periodic
61. In order/ heveled*
62. Shipshape
63. Organized
64. Spic-and-span
65. Systematized
66. Syntax
67. Topsy*

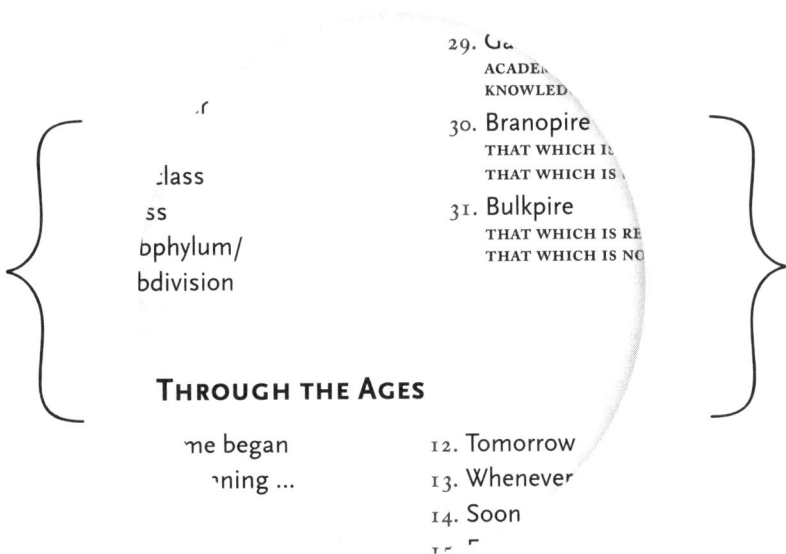

.r

:lass

ss

bphylum/
bdivision

THROUGH THE AGES

Nothing
XXX.1

1. Vacuum
2. Radiation
3. String
4. Quark
5. Electron
6. Proton or neutron
7. Atom
8. Molecule
9. Organic molecule
10. Ribosome
11. Mitochondrion
12. Cell
13. Speck
14. Grain
15. Marble
16. Ball
17. Globe
18. Meteor
19. Asteroid
20. Comet
21. Moon
22. Planet
23. Sun-like star
24. Supergiant
25. Singularity
26. Galactic arm
27. Galaxy core
28. Galaxy core black hole
29. Galaxy
30. Galaxy gobbler
31. Galaxy cluster
32. Supercluster
33. Group
34. Pre-Big Bang origin mass
35. The Bulk

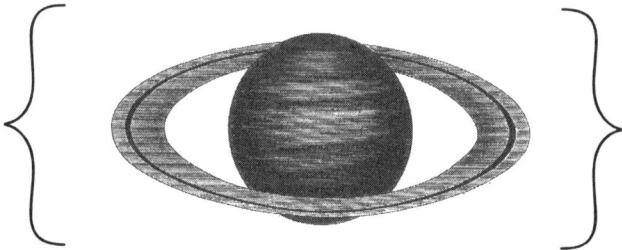

Planet

XXXI.22

GLOSSARY

ABSOLUTE INCREMENT* (Segments of Time) Like frames in a movie, the smallest measurement of time during which the smallest irreducible section of the fastest possible movement can occur in our reality. Scientists, commence bombardment.

AIRMADA* (Military Units in Air) Airmada is to aircraft as armada is to navies.

AIRMAG* (Military Units in Air) Airmag is to aircraft as Armag* is to soldiers.

ALDERAAN* (Degrees of Disaster) Disaster on the scale of the exploding of a planet and the killing of billions. An homage to **[SPOILER ALERT!]** *Star Wars: A New Hope*, in which the home planet of Princess Leia, Alderaan, is destroyed by the Death Star, under the command of Grand Moff Tarkin, as a demonstration of its power.

AMAZILE* (Bodies of Water) A super river, of a magnitude such as the Amazon or Nile.

AN ASIMOV* (Size of Political Entities) A nation whose jurisdiction encompasses all of reality. Named after Isaac Asimov, a font of imagination.

ANNIHILATION OF REALITY* (Degrees of Disaster by Newsworthiness) Our mere universe is contained within existence, which is itself contained within reality. Reality is terminologically distinct from existence in that existence contains all that exists, but reality contains all that really does or does not exist. In the realm of human description, reality is the supreme noun. The annihilation of reality would be the utter voiding of all, but that it had happened would remain, and thus this is just slightly less bad than Nullification of reality*.

ANTIPOTIVE* (Comparison in Groups of Three or More) Absolutely opposed and opposite in every way, as much as is possible in the given sample group.

ANTRIUM* (Shame to Pride) Its definition is best explained by its place on the list. This word began as 'anti-triumph,' was shaved down to 'antriumph,' and finally, the semi-tactile oomph of the ending 'ph' was removed to represent the impact vaccum felt in such places. I think it has a good ring.

AORTA* (Roads by Size) A road from 41 to 80 lanes wide.

APOGEE* (Meetings) Before *Thesaurus of Extremes*, this word was from astronomy, and also used in imagery of high-ness. It is technically the high point of a planetary orbit, higher than a summit, peak, or even a zenith. I propose it as a good name for the eventual 'World Congress' if, at some point, we accomplish a democratic world-state with the power of law. The ultimate Super-Meeting of the species. Or maybe It could be the once-a-year state-of-the-union-type ceremony the World Congress goes through as a celebration of permanent human peace, etc. But no rush.

APOGEEAN* (Shame to Pride) Pretty much as good as it gets pride-wise, within the context of the thus-far-recorded human experience. Like liberating Paris from the Nazis ... single-handedly.

APPRENTIC* (You Did a __ Job) That degree of competence displayed by the winner of a given season of *The Apprentice*. Thousands of talented, ambitious people boil down to one winner, whose 'talent' is simply raw, sharp, indefatigable competence in any of a wide array of tasks.

ARCH-BIBLE* (Scale of Written Composition) Really, really, really big, important book.

ARCH-CODEX* (Scale of Written Composition) A book with more knowledge than most libraries. Requires heavy equipment just to turn the pages, let alone move the whole thing around.

ARCHPIRE* (Size of Political Entities) When we're so far distant from the pre-democratic world that we reach back to the romantic-sounding parts of our past to label our future political constructs, I imagine a '-pire' suffix will suffice to label the increasing scale of that growth. An archpire would compose a whole continent, but in modern democratic control. The EU and the USA both approach this threshold but do not yet cross it.

ARCH-THESIS* (Scale of Written Composition) A work of academic prowess ranking between encyclopedia and treatise, like if you were stuck as an undergraduate student for eight years and had to do something with your time, and it all condensed into one of these.

ARCH-TOME* (Scale of Written Composition) A book, like as if Newton had lived three hundred years, had also completed the work of Maxwell and Einstein all by himself, and then summed it all up in one uber-book. Lift with your legs.

ARCH-TREATISE* (Scale of Written Composition) A book of intimidating weight and comprehensive inclusion. An example would be *Big Red*, a comprehensive book on electromagnetism based on Maxwell's work, or those *Complete Works of Shakespeare* books you can buy.

ARMAG* (Military Units on Land) Derived from *armageddon*, and introducing 'mag' as a suffix describing gargantuan military units. This is the size of armies that would be fighting it out during the prophesized battles described in the Book of Revelation. Composed of tens of millions of soldiers.

ARTIFICIAL MALTACTOPLASTY* (Pleasure to Pain) Mal = bad, tacto = feel, plasty = a surgical procedure. This is a hypothetical, maniacal employment of future technology to torture through direct brain signals and such. Highest possible level of pain without dulling, being kept awake to prevent passing out from pain, etc. Pretty much the worst thing ever.

ATMA-*,** (Prefix Hyperbole) More extreme than eight pallets of Mountain Dew. Transcendent extreme, like a near-omnipotent god who has't gotten SO transcendent as to not care about coming back and showing us how he can wiggle the moon around with his finger. 'Dude! This is awesome! Check it out!' References 'atmaweapon' of *Final Fantasy* fame, the first use of the term as a prefix that I could find, and which itself references 'atman,' a word in both Hinduism and Buddhism that refers to the soul, or true self.

AUGMARK* (Degrees of Disaster by Newsworthiness) Full-on planet collision, aug = create, mark is the term used to describe stages of the Earth's manifestation, acting here as a root word; or, alternatively, Theiaclasm (after the 'Theia' planet which, according to the 'Giant Impact Hypothesis,' collided with early Earth and reformed it). Other alternative names for this awesome (old def.) event could be, after scientists who discovered the collision, perhaps called a Hardavoclasm, or Hardavoclash; Davharclasm; Davharclash. The stages of the Earth's agglomeration before and after this impact are known as 'Earth Mark 1' and 'Earth Mark 2', and so augmark means 'to create a mark.' Should another planet hit us and destroy both, the eventually re-solidified body would be known as 'Earth Mark 3' to survivors.

AUGOCOSMIC* (Candlepower) Aug = to create. Augocosmic means 'as bright as the big bang.' Give or take an order of magnitude.

AUGREAL* (Degrees of Explosion) Big Bang is to our universe as the augreal is to all of reality, which is that larger construct within which our universe is contained.

AUGSCAB* (Degrees of Disaster by Newsworthiness; Bodies of Water) Also known as a Missoula flood, a Spokane Flood, or a Bretz Flood, these are cataclysmic floods of which geologists have found evidence, which occur when gargantuan lakes partially surrounded by ice-dams break free of the ice, and in their calliopic cascade, carve mountains into scab-like shapes which don't otherwise occur in nature. These floods take out entire regions and are, in my opinion, one of the most interesting events in all of geology. See Scabland generator*.

AXIS BRANI* (Classical Architectural Prowess) The manifestation of the classical model as would be expressed when enshrining the central nexus of a Kardashev 5 civilization.

AXIS BULKI* (Classical Architectural Prowess) The manifestation of the classical model as would be expressed when enshrining the central nexus of a Kardashev 6 civilization.

AXIS GALACTI* (Classical Architectural Prowess) The manifestation of the classical model as would be expressed when enshrining the central nexus of a Kardashev 3 civilization.

AXIS REAL* (Classical Architectural Prowess) The manifestation of the classical model as would be expressed when enshrining the central nexus of all of reality. Basically, God's throneroom.

AXIS SOLI* (Classical Architectural Prowess) The manifestation of the classical model as would be expressed when enshrining the central nexus of a Kardashev 2 civilization.

AXIS UNIVERSI* (Classical Architectural Prowess) The manifestation of the classical model as would be expressed when enshrining the central nexus of a Kardashev 4 civilization.

BAND* (The Speed of Multipedal Locomotion) That motion of big cats whose bodies seems to elastically boing into acceleration.

BEHEMOPOLIS* (Urban Growth) Defined by location on list.

BEHEMOTAG* (Military Units on Land) A military unit composed of billions of soldiers. The word derives from the biblical 'Behemoth,' the land-based expression of God's power as described in the Book of Job and existing in a trio of epic beasts along with Ziz, a bird, and the Leviathan, a sea serpent.

BESIC* (Funniness) There are actually very few gods of Humor. The Egyptian god Bes, which among other things represents humor, would, if real, bear a capacity for laughter-inducment that would rise to the level of necessitating quarantine because of the wake of people laughing to death. This word describes a god-level humor impossible to humans. The choice of 'Bes' as a root word I think is appropriate because of a generally light feel and its fantastic brevity.

BILDERBERGOID* (Meetings) A meeting of a plurality or more of important world leaders, but less so than a Grand Terramot*.

Named after the group called 'The Bilderbergers' by conspiracy theorists. Mystery aside, the reality from my research seems to be that this group is basically an institution that arranges private meetings in which numerous powerful cultural, technological, political, and other world leaders can meet and discuss positive change without the glare of media coverage and fear of retribution by their customers or polls if they want to try out and talk about controversial ideas. Within that bubble is a freedom often lost to people who've reached that tier. They wield no official power, and so the transparency I would ordinarily demand of the outcomes of such super-summits is not required. Meet on Bilderbergers; I'm confident you mean well.

BORDER WALL* (Degrees of Barrier) Walls such as those that exist between Palestine and Israel, and are springing up elsewhere.

BORGIC* (Comparison in Groups of Three or More) Distinguishable after brief inspection, but all of a same template. Further defined by location on list, and by the Borg of the *Star Trek* universe.

BRAIGHETORIATE* (Magnitude of Flatulence) Named after the title of professional farters of historical Ireland (braigetori).

BRAIN BUG, ZERG OVERMIND, BORG QUEEN, ETC.** (Rogue's Gallery) A villain on the order of some collective, alien super-intelligence. These are terms from *Starship Troopers*, *Starcraft*, and *Star Trek*, respectively.

BRANCH* (Roads by Size) A road from 161 to 320 lanes wide.

BRANELIFE* (Segments of Time) As yet undetermined average life of a brane, at least in the tens of billions of years, perhaps orders of magnitude larger. Branes are larger-than-universe structures in M-Theory.

BRANIC* (The Significance of Events) An event important enough to effect change across a brane.

BRANOBLINK* (Degrees of Disaster) Disaster on the scale of the blinking out of existence of a brane.

BRANOCALYPSE* (Degrees of Disaster) Disaster on the scale of the violent rending of a brane.

BRANOCLASM* (Degrees of Disaster) Disaster on the scale of the disruption of the structure of a brane.

BRANOCLYSM* (Degrees of Disaster) Disaster on the scale of the breaking up of a brane.

BRANOGRAPHY* (The Size of Writing) Writing composed of entire branes. Branes are larger-than-universe structures in M-Theory.

BRANOLITH* (Sizes of Earth) A rock the size of, or composing, a brane. Not really sure how that would work, though.

BRANOPIRE* (Size of Political Entities) A nation whose jurisdiction encompasses a large chunk of a brane.

BRANOPIRE* (Degrees of Taxonomic Elements) See Panpire a.k.a. plateau*.

BRANOPOLIS* (Urban Growth) A city taking up a large chunk of a brane.

BROWNIC SOLOGRAPHY* (The Size of Writing) References 'Pi in the Sky,' a short story by Fredric Brown, in which stars form an advertisement.

BUKKAKEE* (Chastity) The one upon whom the bukkake is enacted, as opposed to the bukkaker, as indicated by the extra 'e.'

Bulk ocean nullification* (Degrees of Disaster by Newsworthiness) Nullification is the ultimate destruction, destroying not just the memory that a thing exists, but indeed the fact that it actually existed. The bulk ocean is a proposed endless sea of bulks, as described in M-Theory.

Bulkalypse* (Degrees of Disaster) Disaster on the scale of the violent rending of the bulk.

Bulkic* (The Significance of Events) An event of such importance that it effects change across the bulk.

Bulkoblink* (Degrees of Disaster) Disaster on the scale of the blinking out of existence of the bulk.

Bulkoclasm* (Degrees of Disaster) Disaster on the scale of the disruption of the structure of the bulk.

Bulkoclysm* (Degrees of Disaster) Disaster on the scale of the breaking up of the bulk.

Bulkogeddon* (Combat) War across the bulk. Note: All the city-size prefix constructs can be equally applied to the '-geddon' suffix.

Bulkography* (Degrees of the Sizes of Writing) Writing composed of multiple bulks. One bulk being the sum of many branes, as proposed by M-Theory.

Bulkolith* (Sizes of Earth) A rock the size of the bulk, though I'm not sure it really works like that.

Bulkopire* (Size of Political Entities) A nation whose jurisdiction is the bulk.

BULKOPIRE⁎ (Degrees of Taxonomic Elements) See Panpire a.k.a. plateau⁎.

BULKOPOLIS⁎ (Urban Growth) A city the size of the bulk.

BULKOUS⁎ (Object Sizes) As big as the whole bulk.

BULLION⁎ (Degrees of House) To build on my building of 'ingot,' a 'bullion' is any residence with between 100,000,000 and 499,999,999 square feet of indoor space.

BURST⁎ (The Speed of Multipedal Locomotion) The fastest speed among all land animals but for the cheetah. The full-tilt sprint of the savannah.

CACOLYPSE⁎ (Degrees of Disaster) An apocalyptic event caused by malevolent divinity, without the help of benevolent divinity.

CACOMORPHIC⁎ (Chaos and Order) Borrowing the oomph from cacophony, which is a rad word, this word is best understood by its location on the list. It also implies a quality of a thing in violent desperation to constantly destroy and re-form itself and everything around it, as if possessing a will toward chaos.

CALLIOPIC⁎ (The Significance of Events) Basically, it means 'super-epic.' A reference to Calliope, the Greek muse of epic poetry.

CAPTAIN Q⁎ (Rogue's Gallery) Straddling the fence between archetype and cliché, Captain Q is that really mean alpha male on the other team who's better equipped and uniformed than you. He rules his team with a primitive hierarchical social structure and with an iron fist, as does his coach, who is usually just a 20-year-older xerox of Captain Q. Always ready to give an end-of-act-1 scathing insult to our ragtag group of good guys. Captian Q can also be female. (See *Bring It On*.)

CARAT* (Degrees of House) 'Palace' is thus far the highest in the house order; to build on that, I've decided to borrow hierarchical terms describing amounts of gold, as reflects the wealth suggested by such a residence. A carat is a house significantly larger than the Louvre or Versailles, with the Palacio Royal in Madrid and the Imperial Palace in Beijing just barely scraping the bottom end of this one. Expect personal homes on this scale in the next few decades, such is our prosperity.

CARCALLICA* (Classical Architectural Prowess) Only two buildings yet constructed have met this definition in scale: the now-ruined Baths of Carcalla and St. Peter's Basillica in Rome. Monumental grandeur on the scale of stadiums.

CARDINAL PARADIGM* (Certainty) A scientific paradigm which has been repeatedly tested and re-proven so many times as to take on a new hue of absolute as opposed to a relatively new paradigm. The gravitational laws that predict the movements of the planets would be a good example of this, as they have remained mostly unchanged since Isaac Newton.

CARNEGIEL* (Cleverness) Homage to Dale Carnegie, author of the still-popular 1936 best-seller *How to Win Friends and Influence People*.

CATALYPSE* (Degrees of Disaster) An apolcalyptic disaster without divine cause. A meaningless end to the world, like **[SPOILER ALERT!]** what the robots managed to accomplish in the *Matrix* backstory.

CENTILITH* (Sizes of Earth) A hundreth the size of a regular boulder.

CHEET* (The Speed of Multipedal Locomotion) The fastest a cheetah can go. It's worth noting that the cheetah is the world's fastest land animal, and thus, this is the fastest naturally occurring speed of multipedal locomotion in the animal kingdom, clocked at well over sixty miles per hour.

CHRONOTANGENTIAL* (Segments of Time) A hunk of time so massive it breaks loose of the 2D arrow of time and bends off in other directions. I have absolutely no clue if this has any bearing on reality, but I think the word is a pretty fun one.

CLICKER, THE* (Rogue's Gallery) That mysterious lurking threat unseen but for first-person POV, briefly caught in shadows and reflections, until finally and disappointingly revealed to be some conglomeration of all-too-familiar organic or doll parts. Lame.

COALITION OF THE WILLING* (Party Formality) A room of adults with the gumption and attractiveness to create an atmosphere where everyone is pretty much attracted to everyone else, and so exists a fertile soil for debauchery. The arrangement of drink and people adds a subtext of sexual potentiality to the whole evening. Or so I've heard.

COGNOSCENTE* (Degrees of Academic Degrees) An already-existing word referring to deep, committed knowledge in an area, and here re-applied to specifically describe the next step up from doctorate. This new application comes from the fictional universe of *The Great Beyond* (see Great Beyond, The*). Specifically, in that universe, 'cognoscente' is an academic rank earned after earning six Ph.D.s, and then pulling from all of that knowledge to produce a 'cognoscente arch-thesis' (like a doctoral dissertation). A university is different from a college in that it offers PhDs. The institution which offers cognoscente degrees ought to be known as an 'aristarchus,' after the renowned librarian of the ancient library of Alexandria. See also Eruditor* and Sophic*.

COLONEL DOMUS* (Degrees of Male House Staff) Building off the 'Major Domus' prior, this follows the implied military officer hierarchy from 'Chain of Command.'

CONPULL* (Degrees of Conpull) That thus-far-unnamed catergory into which wire, string, twine, cable, climbers' webbing, chain, rope, line, and the like all fit into. You know what I mean. I checked, and there's no word for that. This is it. Conpull is a portmandeau of 'connect' and 'pull,' the two purposes of these devices. The end.

CONTINOPOLIS* (Urban Growth) A contiguous city filling out the better part of a continent.

COPROPHAGIAN* (Disgusting to Delicious) Building on 'coprophagia,' a word that means eating poo.

COSMOGRAPHY* (The Size of Writing) Writing composed of cosmoses.

DAMNATIO MEMORIAE* (Insult to Praise) The man who burnt down the Temple of Artemis, one of the wonders of the ancient world, declared he did so so that history would remember his name. The city leaders declared that anyone mentioning his name would be put to death. No, I'm not going to tell you his name. A similar story is attached to the murderer of Buffalo Bill. When the Roman Senate enacted this tradition, the names of the persons were scratched from buildings and temples, their statues demolished, and any other record of their existence, destroyed. This is the ultimate capacity of human institutions to insult.

DEAD-OF-NIGHT BITE* (Times to Eat) A meal eaten in the dead of night. It's a little kitschy, with an unfortunate zombie aftertaste, but it rhymes, so I'm going with it.

DECILITH* (Sizes of Earth) A hunk of earth about one-tenth the size of your average boulder.

DEMIURGIC* (Creativity) Demiurge, from Plato, means 'Prime Mover,' i.e., the uncreated creator. An entity capable of manifesting the universe, or even all of reality, out of nothing. Think about it; not only would they have to conceive of the act of creating anything at all, but then conceive the means, the idea of forms and structure, and then of executing a form, and a structure. An entity which would have to 'think up' details like 'time' and 'space,' 'cause' and 'effect,' etc. After that, it would design a universe which would occupy that time and space. From absolute void. That's a significant level of creative will and capacity.

DIPOCALYPSE* (Degrees of Disaster) An apocalyptic event on two worlds.

DIVINANT* (Contractual Agreements) An agreement between gods, but less than omnipotent gods, such as might exist between Zeus and Neptune.

DRIPLET* (Bodies of Water) Drop is to droplet as drip is to driplet. Since a drop is bigger than a drip, driplet is smaller than a droplet.

DRIZZLET* (Bodies of Water) A gathering of water the size of a single unit of drizzle.

DWINELLE* (Maze Difficulty) Named after the grossly overcomplicated construction of Dwinelle Hall on the campus of UC Berkeley. Navigating these halls is sadly the only remnant left of the once-proud freshman hazing rituals at Cal.

DYSON SPHERE** (Size of Political Entities) A structure that completely surrounds a star and captures all of its outgoing energy. When first constructed, I imagine this will be the residence of the bulk of the body politic itself.

DYSON SWARM** (Size of Political Entities) Less complete than a dyson sphere; still, a swarm of craft partially surrounding a star would surely be home to trillions and, in the distant future of space colonization, might very well often form unto itself a closed political entity. Maybe.

ECUMENOPIRE* (Size of Political Entities) A complete, democratic, one-world government, borrowing from ecumenopolis, which builds on the 'ecumenical'o suffix, which is derived from the Greek *oikoumene*, which means 'the inhabited world.'

ECUMENOPOLIS** (Urban Growth) A city, such as Corsucant or Trantor, that takes up the entire surface of a planet. A term coined by Constantinos Doxiadis. An ecumenopolis would almost always, but not necessarily, constitute a Kardashev 1 civilization.

EDISONIAN* (Creativity) This word describes an incredible, once-in-an-age fountain of new. Referencing Thomas Edison, the 'Wizard of Menlo Park,' who was responsible for thousands of inventions and for a greater improvement in human life than perhaps any single person in the last two centuries. The ubiquitous convenience of electricity in our world exists as we know it because of this man. There are 1,097 patents in his name.

EFFLUVIOUS* (Disgusting to Delicious) Effluvium is the liquid which forms, under proper conditions, of the decomposition of flesh. I'm gonna go wash my hands now.

ELBOW-LIFTING* (Candlepower) So bright, holding your hand up doesn't block the light enough, and you have to bury your eyes into your elbow to protect them. As a sidenote, if you ever get jumped, burying your nose into your elbow while curled up will help protect most of your face from kicks and blows.

EMPEROR SIZE* (Chocolate Bar Sizes) Emperor is to king as Emperor Size is to King Size.

EMPYREAN* (Shame to Pride) Empyrean already refers to having to do with the sky. In this application, it refers to a proud feeling which might be described visually as looking like skipping between nebulas at superluminal speed, but which is simultaneously grounded in mighty achievement.

ENCYCLOPEDIA GALACTICA** (Scale of Written Composition) The concept of an 'Encyclopedia Galactica' was proposed by Carl Sagan and describes a vast galactic store of the knowledge of perhaps thousands of intelligent species combined for shared use. A book containing this much knowledge would be of epic scale. You could play football on it.

ENORMOPOLIS* (Urban Growth) Defined by location on list.

EPICER* (Introduction) More epic. Totally a word.

EPT* (You Did a __ Job) Inept is a word, but thus far ept isn't. So since inept means 'lacking aptitude,' ept, as implied by the prefix, would be a degree of aptitude between premium and special. Apt is to intelligence as ept is to competence.

ERUDITOR* (Degrees of Academic Degrees) An academic degree one rank higher than Cognoscente*. Institutions which offer eruditors I propose should be called an 'apollo' after the Greek god of learning. See also Cognoscente* and Sophic*. Bachelor's Degree < Doctorate < Cognoscente < Eruditor < Sophic.

ESCHER NIGHTMARE* (Maze Difficulty) Imagine the worst nightmare M.C. Esher might be capable of, as expressed in his uniquely talented 3D visualization capacity, and as a maze. Wowsers.

EXALITH* (Sizes of Earth) A hunk of earth roughly around the size of a quintillion of your average boulders.

EXANNUM* (Segments of Time) A quintillion, or 1,000,000,000,000,000,000 years.

EXTROPIC* (Degrees of Normal and Strange) Extropy is the notion of a positive, reasoned, human populating of the universe through technology and in peace. Perhaps immortal. It's a nice thought, actually. I put it here on this list so that such an alien concept might, through word association, be brought closer to the center of expectation. It is thus re-applied here as a word meaning 'very normal, almost certainly going to happen.'

FEMTOLITH* (Sizes of Earth) One-quadrillionth of a normal-sized boulder.

FIVE-DOG NIGHT** (Temperature by Degrees) Borrowed from sled-dog slang and meaning so cold that surviving the night would require the combined body heat of five sled dogs.

FLASH* (The Speed of Multipedal Locomotion) That running speed attained by the several superheroes with the gift of extreme running speed.

FOUR-DOG NIGHT** (Temperature by Degrees) Borrowed from sled-dog slang and meaning so cold that surviving the night would require the combined body heat of four sled dogs.

FRYSOLOGRAPHY* (The Size of Writing) In an episode of *Futurama*, the main character, Fry, arranges stars into a love note. This word describes such an act.

FUZZY CRUST/FUZZY PLANET* (Quantities of Wood) Enough forest to make a planet discernibly fuzzy to a hand which could hold it.

GABOPREXY* (Resentment to Gratitude) Super-appreciation. This one is pure id-babble.

GALACTOBLINK* (Degrees of Disaster) Disaster on the scale of the blinking out of existence of an entire galaxy.

GALACTOCLASM✷ (Degrees of Disaster) Disaster on the scale of the disruption of the structure of a galaxy.

GALACTOCLYPSE✷ (Degrees of Disaster) Disaster on the scale of the violent rending of a galaxy.

GALACTOCLYSM✷ (Degrees of Disaster) Disaster on the scale of the breaking up of a galaxy.

GALACTOGEDDON✷ (Combat) War across a large chunk of a galaxy.

GALACTOLITH✷ (Sizes of Earth) A galaxy-sized rock.

GALACTOPIRE✷ (Size of Political Entities) A nation taking up a large chunk of a galaxy.

GALACTOPIRE✷ (Degrees of Taxonomic Elements) See Panpire a.k.a. plateau*.

GALACTOPOLIS✷ (Urban Growth) A city reaching across a large chunk of a galaxy.

GALAXOGRAPHY✷ (The Size of Writing) Writing composed of galaxies.

GARGANTOPOLIS✷ (Urban Growth) Defined by location on list.

GATE GENERATOR✷ (Degrees of Disaster) Beginning with Watergate, a number of scandals have taken on the 'gate' suffix to mean a politically disadvantageous event or situation approaching the scale of the Watergate scandal. Examples include 'Monicagate' and 'Travelgate,' among many others. The magnitude required to achieve 'gate' status has, however, been diluted as time passes, and so the suffix has come to mean simply 'political scandal,' but of a variety of magnitudes.

GENERAL DOMUS✼ (Degrees of Male House Staff) Building off the 'Major Domus' prior, this follows the implied military officer hierarchy.

GEOBLINK✼ (Degrees of Disaster) Disaster on the scale of the blinking of a planet out of existence.

GEOCALYPSE✼ (Degrees of Disaster) Disaster on the scale of the disruption of the structure of a planet so profound its original shape and arrangement of the parts are indiscernible without serious study.

GEOCLASM✼ (Degrees of Disaster) Disaster on the scale of the breaking up of not just the crust, but the internal structure of a planet.

GEOCLYSM✼ (Degrees of Disaster) Destruction on the scale of the breaking up of a whole planet.

GEOPOLIS✼ (Urban Growth) A city taking up the better part of the whole surface of the planet, including water area.

GIGABRANOPIRE✼ (Size of Political Entities) A nation whose jurisdiction encompasses between 1,000,000,000 and 999,999,999,999 branes.

GIGABRANOPOLIS✼ (Urban Growth) A city taking up between 1,000,000,000 and 999,999,999,999 branes.

GIGAGALACTOPIRE✼ (Size of Political Entities) A nation whose jurisdiction encompasses between 1,000,000,000 and 999,999,999 galaxies.

GIGAGALACTOPOLIS✼ (Urban Growth) A city taking up between 1,000,000,000 and 999,999,999,999 galaxies.

GIGALITH✼ (Sizes of Earth) A hunk of earth around the size of a billion of your average boulders.

GIGALOPOLIS✻ (Urban Growth) Defined by location on list. In this case, the metric prefix doesn't necessarily numerically apply, but is being drawn more from the vein of prefix hyperbole.

GIGASOLAPIRE✻ (Size of Political Entities) A nation spanning from 1,000,000,000 to 999,999,999,999 stars.

GIGASOLAPOLIS✻ (Urban Growth) A city spanning from 1,000,000,000 to 999,999,999,999 stars.

GINNUNGAGAP✻ (Degrees of Barrier; Degress of Fissure) Much like the waters mentioned in the first paragraph of Genesis, or the Brahman of Hinduism, this is the gap of epic absence in which the world was created in Nordic mythology.

GLACIOPOLIS✻ (Urban Growth) Defined by location on list.

GOD SPEED✻ (The Rate of Speed) The top speed of God. Basically, infinity fast. Also, a fun play on words.

GOLGOTHIC/BODHIC/HIRIC/SINAIC✻ (The Significance of Events) The most important events in history are arguably the crucial moments in the stories of the founders of the great religions, such as the death and resurrection of Jesus, the transcendence of Buddha under the Bodhi Tree, the receiving of the ten commandments atop Mt. Sinai by Moses, and the revelations to Muhammad in the caves of the mountains of Hira. Historically, periods of time separated by such events are called 'epochs,' and in terms of this list, an event of such importance already falls under the definition of 'epochal.' See Nexus protagonist✻.

GOOGOLMETER✻ (The Distance Between Two Points) A googol meters.

GOOGOLPARSEC✻ (The Distance Between Two Points) A googol parsecs.

GOOGOLPLEXOMETER* (The Distance Between Two Points) A googolplex meters.

GOOGOLPLEXOPARSEC* (The Distance Between Two Points) A googolplex parsecs.

GORDION HALLWAY* (Maze Difficulty) Maze with confusion on the level that it would look like the Gordion knot were built on a gigantic scale and composed of hallways instead of rope, but all interconnected, not just one long line.

GORGY* (Meal Size) Portmandeau of gorge and orgy. A ridiculous, over-the-top indulgence in flavor and quantity.

GRAKKAW* (Degrees of Normal and Strange) That perfect, impossible magnitude of strangeness we humans lack the capacity to imagine, and which the gods in their wisdom don't share.

GRAND TERRAMOT* (Meetings) A meeting of world leaders in which well over 90 percent of the world's population is represented, such as might happen at the UN if aliens arrived, etc. A 'special assembly' of the United Nations Security Council, when all the heads of state show up, doesn't quite count as a meeting of this order, as the outcome bears no legal power. A prerequisite of a Grand Terramot would be that it would have binding legal force. The construction of the word itself is about half id-babble; I just thought it up and thought it sounded good. The 'terra' refers to Earth, and the 'grand' just gives it bonus oomph.

GRBIC* (Candlepower) As bright as a gamma-ray burst. Gamma-ray bursts are more powerful than supernovas. They are the brightest known cosmic events since the Big Bang.

GRB-OGRAPHY* (The Size of Writing) Writing composed of GRBs, or gamma-ray bursts, cosmic super-explosions more powerful than supernovas.

GREAT BEYOND, THE* It's a 342-page distant-future-epic script by this book's author, set in a completely fictional universe constructed by the same, which flips the Dystopian cliché on its head. Here's the pitch: The story is about a hunted hunter-gatherer aware only of his nasty, brutish, and short life, who, believing he has been killed, is illegally lifted from the Amazon Feral Reserve by invisible forces into the beautiful paradise of immortal godlike luxury that occupies the rest of the surface of our planet. Once there, he must find a way back to his jungle home to save the sons in danger he left behind. The motives behind his extraction, which is in violation of the World Constitution of 2500, and how it could possibly have been achieved without government detection, are the major mysteries which will, by the end, be solved. Are you reading this James Cameron, Peter Jackson, George Lucas, and Steven Spielberg? If you love *ToE*, you'll *adore The Great Beyond*. Let the bidding war begin.

GUINESSACK* (Meal Size) There are dozens of Guiness Book of World Records records which describe the creation of some largest ever culinary creation, such as 'World's Largest Pie,' etc. This word describes the meal after. The 'sack' runs off the root word well and implies the stomach and its fullness.

GYGO-* (Prefix Hyperbole) Best indicated by location of list. Extremely ultra, a reference to Gygo, the largest among the strongest entities in the Greek pantheon, the Hecatonchieres. Even stronger than the gods and titans, the Hecatonchieres had a hundred hands, and with each, they could throw a mountain.

HADEAN* (Through the Ages) 140 or older. Refers to the Hadean Geologic Eon, which ended 3.8 billion years ago.

HALF-SLEW, A* (Non-Numerical Elastic Quantities) A whole slew divided by two.

HAND-LIFTING* (Candlepower) So bright that closing your eyes doesn't do the trick, and you have to hold your hand up to block the light.

HAPPY BUTTON* (Illicitness of Drug) Inspired by a 1954 experiment by James Olds and Peter Milner, this phrase describes a form of direct-brain-stimulation ideally designed to create a sense of artificial happiness more powerful even than heroin. Such a technology would be so ridiculously euphoric, it could in the future prove a more illicit 'drug' than any available today. Such a device would be capable of destroying all capacity for joy besides itself. See also Artificial Maltactoplasty*.

HARD GALAXY* (Degrees of Fortification) A fortification wielding the collective size and power of a galaxy toward its protection from outside threat. A solid object upwards of 100,000 light years or more across. Perhaps a sagacious future construct, or perhaps a malignancy of some future ultra-malithogog*.

HARD PLANET* (Degrees of Fortification) A fortification composing a whole planet. Cement and steel, or maybe something harder, deep through to the core. Plenty of lasers and stuff, too.

HARD STAR* (Degrees of Fortification) A fortification composing a whole star or bigger. Probably with the star still burning within, and the energy transferred to guns, and long-term energy stores to survive aeons-long sieges.

HEEPODOO* (Resentment to Gratitude) Constructed of more id-babble. An emotion of gratitude so extreme, it doesn't occur in nature. Beyond the human experience thus far. The kind of gratitude a soul might feel after being freed from hell after a few billion years in one of those lakes of fire.

HELEN* (Military Units on Water or in Space) A Helen, named after the woman whose face 'launched a thousand ships,' describes a naval source on the scale of the 'Operation Downfall' force that was all ready to invade Japan before their surrender in 1945. For comparison, Douglass MacCarthur, who was to command the invasion, might very well have been promoted to a six-star 'General of the Armies' prior to the invasion.

HELTER* (Chaos and Order) Helter-skelter minus the skelter, so, less messy.

HEVELED* (Chaos and Order) Disheveled is to heveled as disordered is to ordered.

HISTORIC EON* (Segments of Time) See Historic era*.

HISTORIC ERA* (Segments of Time) My research of timescales seems to imply a hierarchy as follows: Epoch < Period < Age < Era < Eon, Eon being the longest; and also Historic < Geologic < Cosmic. So the various combinations of all these terms are ranked appropriately by their definitions, as best as I could determine. As far as I can tell, historic era and historic eon are unused. We probably don't even really need them yet, but recorded history has a lot of time ahead of itself, so these are in anticipation of future catergorizations including vast periods of recorded, and as-yet-unrecorded history.

HOLY LIVING FUCK** (Degrees of Warning/Caution/Danger) From July 21, 1969, moon landing headline from *The Onion*. According to the article, these were Neil Armstrong's first words as he set foot on the moon.

HOME* (Degrees of House) All the square footage in the world can't make a house a home, only love can ... I think I read that somewhere embroidered in a frame.

HUMONGOPOLIS* (Urban Growth) Defined by location on list.

HYPERCOGITATIVE* (Intelligence) A level of intelligence beyond the capacity of our species, limited to divinity, ridiculously intelligent computers, aliens, or maybe some super-pimped-out future transhuman version of ourselves.

HYPERGABOPREXY* (Resentment to Gratitude) Extremely appreciative. See Gaboprexy*.

HYPERLAMBENT* (Candlepower) Violently bright. A deluge of photons that can tear down a mountain range.

IBMIGRAPHY** (The Size of Writing) IBM proved their ability to manipulate individual atoms' positions by aligning them into spelling IBM from thirty-five individual and visible atoms. Acccording to IBM's Web site, this was the first structure ever made out of individual atoms. Ibmigraphy is any writing small enough so that, within the scale of readability, you can see the individual atoms.

-IC* (overused suffix throughout *ToE*) Although I've employed many suffixes, this one is my favorite. I believe in it. It's short, sharp, easy to pronounce, and eager to be paired into homage. Also, as the word epic ends in '-ic,' and many of the new words in this book are at extremes, that suggests an appropriate association.

ICHOROUS* (Disgusting to Delicious) Something that tastes as good as the Ichor of the gods.

ID SLAVE* (Intensity of Feeling) Our id-instincts have base responses ready to serve up for just about every life situation. This word describes a person who has reverted to acting on these impulses without further cognitive digestion and discernment before choosing words or behaviors. It's both easy, and a loss of control.

INFINITESIMETER (A.K.A. ZENOMETER)✲ (The Distance Between Two Points) Basically a meter divided by infinity. Which is totally legitimate math. Totally. Alternatively a Zenometer✲ after Zeno and his Race Course paradox.

INGOT✲ (Degrees of House) To build on my building of 'carat,' an 'ingot' is any residence with between 20,000,000 and 99,999,999 square feet of indoor space.

INCOMPREHENSIBLE✲ (Bad to Good) So bad you can't even comprehend it. A new application of a previously existing word. I was almost certain this word had been used to describe evil before, but no dictionary listed any malevolence under its definition. Dibs!

INDEX GENERATOR✲ (Degrees of Disaster) Tornadoes, hurricanes, and volcanic eruptions all have indices which indicate the magnitude of the event. An index generator is any repeating natural phenomena which sufficiently disrupts human civilization so as to require such an index for the purpose of useful catergorization to handle the effects of the disaster.

INFINIMETER, INIFNIPARSEC, INFINIÅNGSTRÖM, ETC.✲ (The Distance Between Two Points) The unit of measurement means less than the prefix. They are all identically infinite.

INNUOT✲ (Resentment to Gratitude) Id-babble which, in retrospect, I think has something to do with how grateful that Eskimo looks on the tail of the Alaska Airlines jets. The ending also has an absolute conclusiveness to it. This isn't just charity-luncheon-speech gratitude but deep, person-to-person thanks. Beyond hypergaboprexy. This one also introduces the '-uot' suffix, which suggests extreme emotional depth, with just a touch of clinical aura.

INTERDIMENSIONAL* (Object Size) Big enough to take up multiple dimensions.

JAKE* (Shades of Anger) Great friend and angriest man I've ever met, whose full name will go unwritten. Hi, Jake! I hope you're not ironically mad I put you at the top of this list.

JARETH* (Maze Difficulty) A mighty maze named after Jareth, the main villain in *Labyrinth*.

JARJARIC**,* (Bad to Good) Homage, no, heteramage to Jarjar Binks of *Star Wars: Episode One*. *Star Wars* is SO awesome, but this abomination is the bull in the china shop of an otherwise once-in-a-generation, paragon movie franchise. There are worse characters out there, but the juxtaposition with what is otherwise high art, and the sheer collective angst of the viewers toward this entity, is an untapped emotional potentiality here exploited for definition oomph. We all make mistakes, and in fairness, Lucas gave a great rebuttal to our criticism: 'The movies are for children but they don't want to admit that ... There is a small group of fans that do not like comic sidekicks. They want the films to be tough like *The Terminator*, and they get very upset and opinionated about anything that has anything to do with being childlike.'

JORGA-* (Prefix Hyperbole) Super Ultra Mega Extreme to the Max. References Jorgamandr, the world serpent of Norse Mythology, a worm large enough to encircle all the world.

JOVIAN* (Object Sizes) As big as the gas giants beyond the asteroid belt.

JOVIOCEAN* (Bodies of Water) The amount of water that would be required to demonstrate the low density of Saturn by showing how it could float. This is derived from a commonly used analogy in astronomy 101 courses nationwide.

KARDASHEV CIVILIZATIONS 1 THROUGH 6* (Urban Growth, Size of Political Entities) Designed by Nikolai Kardashev, the Kardashev scale describes city and civilization growth on a scale measuring energy use. Kardashev 1 describes a civilization using all the available energy on a single planet; Kardashev 2, all the available energy from a star; Kardashev 3, from a whole galaxy. Building on this, I propose that 4, 5, and 6 should be defined as using all the available energy in a universe, brane, and bulk, respectively.

KARDASHEV RESERVOIR* (Degrees of Ice) As we colonize whole galaxies, a really cool way to store ice might be to just stick it out in space, let it freeze, and then hold on to it, so it wouldn't go anywhere and just sit there floating as this astronomical chunk. In the distant future, such reserves could span thousands of star systems, you know, just to be safe.

KEEPING YOUR HEAD WHEN ALL ABOUT YOU ARE LOSING THEIRS** (Shades of Anger) Inspired by my favorite line from a gorgeous poem by Rudyard Kipling called 'If.' Refers to that state of mind of awareness pursuant to action, combined with calm and grit, basically like that one guy who's not panicking in the panic-worthy situation. The ideal to seek in extreme situations, to best prevent a *Lord of the Flies*-type scenario. If you're ever in a situation like this, I beg you, be this person.

KILOBRANOPIRE* (Size of Political Entities) A nation whose jurisdiction encompasses between 1,000 and 999,999 branes.

KILOBRANOPOLIS* (Urban Growth) A city spanning a thousand or more branes.

KILOGALACTOPIRE* (Size of Political Entities) A nation whose jurisdiction includes between 1,000 and 999,999 galaxies.

KILOGALACTOPOLIS* (Urban Growth) A city spanning a thousand or more galaxies.

KILOSOLAPIRE* (Size of Political Entities) A nation composed of between 1,000 and 999,999 star systems.

KILOSOLAPOLIS* (Urban Growth) A city spanning a thousand or more stars.

KIP* (Times to Eat) What you eat while out late drinking. An homage to Kip's, a beloved local bar at UC Berkeley, where (when I left Cal) for $20, you could get two pitchers, two slices of pizza, and also cover tax and tip.

LANTERNIC* (Candlepower) As bright as your average lantern.

LAPLADEX* (Scale of Written Composition) A book containing the knowledge of two things: the current properties of every quality of reality, i.e. the state of all that exists without exception; and a knowledge of all physical laws that govern the actions of that which exists in the current state. This would give the bearer the ability to predict the future and describe the past with absolute precision. The existence of such a knowledge would at once solve all mysteries and annul free will. The name derives from 'Laplace's Demon,' a philosophical construct of Pierre-Simon Laplace, which bears the quality of knowing both all things which currently exist, and the physical laws which govern their behavior.

LARSON* (Land Surrounded by Water) A tiny mound of sand, with a single palm tree, in the middle of the ocean. Oft-featured in Gary Larson's *The Far Side* comic. *Far Side* really was the best comic ever, but people forget that. Like, no one expected a comic to rise to that level, but wow, Larson really did it.

LEACHATIC* (Disgusting to Delicious) Leachite, which this word is a reference to, is that substance which pools at the bottom of landfills after years of filtering and fermenting between the mentionable and unmentionable disposables which define its mass.

LECTERIC** (Bad to Good) An homage to one of the most memorable movie villains: Dr. Hannibal 'The Cannibal' Lecter from *The Silence of the Lambs*.

LERVE** (Hate to Love) See Luff**; *Annie Hall*.

LEVIANOPOLIS* (Urban Growth) Defined by location on list.

LEVIATAG* (Military Units on Water or in Space) As we eventually go a'colonizing across the universe, we'll need terms to describe the jovian forces which protect those settlers from who-knows-what, and hopefully never turn against each other. This is the bottom of that as-yet-unwritten scale extension. This one seems really important, so as I'm lacking an extensive knowledge of sci-fi literature, I'm open to suggestions from nerds and military folks alike. See Behemotag*, Ziztag*.

LUFF** (Hate to Love) From Woody Allen's *Annie Hall*: 'Love is too weak a word for what I feel. I luuurve you, you know, I loave you, I luff you, two f's, yes I have to invent, of course I - I do, don't you think I do?'

MACRODIMENSIONAL* (Object Sizes) Bigger than a dimension.

MAGINOT* (Degrees of Fortification) A fortification spanning a whole region, on the scale of the Maginot Line built by France between World War I and World War II.

MAJOR DOMA* (Degrees of Female House Staff) Female equivalent of Major Domus in 'Degrees of Male House Staff.'

MALITHOGOG* (Rogue's Gallery) That tyrannical entity that occupies the supreme evil in so many important stories, but with relevant manifestations in real life. Following the standard 'Dicatorship for Dummies' stages of control, the malithogog begins with a perfectly good republic or otherwise peaceful kingdom, takes control by creating an inside or outside enemy, and then, once in control, maintains that control through artificial urgency of extra-state and intra-state threat (and, in fiction, almost always wears black). Defined by rule through fear and decrease in rights and almost always accompanied by some kind of secret police. Military parades are huge and common. Fictional examples are Palpatine (*Star Wars*), Galbatorix (*Eragon*), Saruman (*The Lord of the Rings*), Xerxes (*300*), and in real life Draco, Stalin, Hitler, Mussolini, Saddam Hussein, Kim Jong-Il, and many others. I'd normally call this a cliché, but it's an all-too-real and repeating human threat from within that, so long as we are us, will have potential for punching through into history again. It's definitely worth keeping the 'Beware' sign up by repeating this archetype in our storytelling. Expect a thorough explanation of this archetype in a book from this author in a 'how-to' format in the next few years. 'Mal' = bad, 'lith' = Rock, 'gog' borrowed from 'Demigog,' which is a word with a definition which overlaps this one, but not completely. Malithogog is distinct from a demigog in that a demigog's power is based in the emotion of their followers, whereas a Malithogog can also rule by bringing out the cold logic in his followers, bidding them tip the balance too far in the other direction, and become a glacial voting block, or simply rule by raw, perhaps robotic force without public support.

MARSHAL DOMUS* (Degrees of Male House Staff; Degrees of Female House Staff) Building off the 'Major Domus' prior, this follows the implied military officer hierarchy. See 'Chain of Command.'

MAURADIAN✲ (Through the Ages) Over 130 years of age. An homage to Armen Mauradian, a guy in my fraternity who pledged at the ripe old age of 26. This is anachronistically old for pledging, and this same anachronism on life-scale is thus analogously applied. Hi, Armen!

MEGABRANOPIRE✲ (Size of Political Entities) A nation whose jurisdiction encompasses between 1,000,000 and 999,999,999 branes.

MEGABRANOPOLIS✲ (Urban Growth) A city spanning from 1,000,000 to 999,999,999 branes.

MEGAGALACTOPIRE✲ (Size of Political Entities) a nation whose jurisdiction encompasses between 1,000,000 and 999,999,999 galaxies.

MEGAGALACTOPOLIS✲ (Urban Growth) A city spanning from 1,000,000 to 999,999,999 galaxies.

MEGASOLAPIRE✲ (Size of Political Entities) A nation spanning from 1,000,000 to 999,999,999 stars.

MEGASOLAPOLIS✲ (Urban Growth) A city spanning from 1,000,000 to 999,999,999 stars.

MENGELIC✲ (Bad to Good) Reference to a Nazi human experimenter at Auschwitz who deserves no further explanation.

METEOR DEFENSE COMPLEX✲ (Degrees of Fortification) An apparatus capable of defending a planet from meteors. Probably some combination of detection, banks of computers to track and follow objects, and the capacity to neutralize any threats through a number of different means. Basically, what we should have had ready at the beginning of *Armageddon*, the movie.

MICHAEL HATCH* (Coolness) Defined by location on list.

MICROLITH* (Sizes of Earth) One-millionth the size of a regular boulder.

MIIKEAN* (Disgusting to Delicious) An homage to Takashi Miike, a Japanese director controversial for his use of gore and torture.

MILLILITH* (Sizes of Earth) One-thousandth the size of a regular boulder.

MONK GIGGLY* (Hollowness to Fullfillment) What we imagine those always-laughing buddhist monks must feel like all the time. Whether or not the emotion we imagine is the constant truth of their experience, though they do seem pretty happy, this word describes that sense of wholeness, as we regular folk imagine them feeling it.

MOON ANCHOR* (Degrees of Conpull*) A hypergargantuan segment of Conpull* capable of binding the moon in place to the earth. Just in case.

MOSCHITIC* (Talkativeness) John 'Mightymouth' Moschitta is most well known as the lightning-tongued Micro Machines announcer, and the voice of 'Blurr' in *Transformers: The Movie*. This word refers to a speed of talking as fast as this particular talent.

MULTIBRANOPIRE* (Size of Political Entities) A nation whose jurisdiction encompasses many branes.

MULTIBRANOPOLIS* (Urban Growth) A city taking up many branes.

MULTIGALACTOGEDDON* (Combat) War across many galaxies.

MULTIGALACTOPIRE* (Size of Political Entities) A nation whose jurisdiction encompasses many galaxies.

MULTIGALACTOPOLIS✻ (Urban Growth) A city spanning many galaxies.

MULTIGEDDON✻ (Combat) Combat on the scale of multiple armageddons. As if all the gods of each religion's end-of-the-world scenario showed up all at once, and fought it out with each other for the eternal fate of their followers.

MULTIGEOPIRE✻ (Size of Political Entities) A nation spread across many worlds.

MULTIGEOPOLIS✻ (Urban Growth) A city covering many planets.

MULTISOLAPIRE✻ (Size of Political Entities) A nation reaching across many star systems.

MULTISOLAPOLIS✻ (Urban Growth) A city spanning many star systems.

MULTIUNIVEGEDDON✻ (Combat) War across many universes.

MULTOCALYSPE✻ (Degrees of Disaster) An apocalyptic event on many worlds.

MUNSON✻✻ (Failure to Success) Homage to the move *Kingpin*, where the protagonist, Roy Munson, after losing his good bowling hand in a botched attempt to hustle some thugs, years later learns that because of that event, the local Amish, among others, have incorporated 'Pull a Munson' into their lexicon as meaning: 'You know, Munsoned ... to have the whole world in the palm of your hand and then blow it. It's a figure of speech.' Good movie.

NADIRAL ANTRIUM✻ (Shame to Pride) This phrase describes a sense of such complete, absolute, every-cell-nucleus-penetrating shame that an act of suicide seems a glorious escape, and the thought of it occupies every brain cell not overcome with the sheer fullness of the ignominy itself. Like you might feel like if you accidentally sold out humanity to aliens, who then proceeded to enslave and/or kill off the whole species. 'Antrium' is explaned in its own entry, and 'nadir' is a word that means, as referenced in this particular case, that lowest place in any given cosmogony, such as Tartarus, Dante's ninth circle of Hell, or Groening's Middle School.

Nanolith* (Sizes of Earth) One-billionth the size of a regular boulder.

Nauseous mortification* (Shame to Pride) So ashamed you feel like you're going to puke.

Navada* (Military Units on Land) Navada is to army as armada is to navy. Check out the swapped prefixes. A navada would be composed of millions of soldiers.

Nexus protagonist* (Top Ranks of the Old World) A crucial religious or cultural figure who exists at the nexus of the beginning of a world-scale religion or culture and is wrapped in a heroic tale, such as Aeneas, Abraham, Muhammad, Buddha, Jesus, Marduk, and Harry Stamper (see Stamper*).

Niagaric* (Talkativeness) If words fell like water, this speed of talking would look like Niagara Falls.

Norad* (Degrees of Fortification) NORAD, an acronym for the North American Aerospace Defense Command, includes not just the famed super-bunker at the Cheyenne Mountain Complex but also the entire continental air defense matrix. As used here, this word describes a comprehensive air-defense apparatus for a continent sized area.

Nullification of reality* (Degrees of Disaster by Newsworthiness) Our mere universe is contained within existence, which is itself contained within reality. Reality is terminologically distinct from existence in that existence contains all that exists, but reality contains all that really does or does not exist. In the realm of human description, reality is the supreme noun. The nullification of reality is the absolute worst event possible, indicating not only the blinking out of all, but also the blinking out that it either ever was or wasn't.

NUMBING STUPEFACTION* (Shame to Pride) A level of shame that, after being recovered from, still leaves an indelible, cynical scar on what remains of the feeler's childlike bubbly. Numbs you just a little bit to the world. Stupefaction is that state of shock at a thing that leaves one briefly dumber.

OKINAWIC* (Through the Ages) Anyone over 120 years of age. Refers to Okinawa, an island known for the statistical longetivity of its residents.

OMERTIC* (Talkativeness) Absolute, and also unbreakable, silence. An homage to the oath of silence widely known as a part of Mafia lore. Also, there is no Mafia, but if there were one in real life, I'd bet they'd have an oath like that too. This colloquial use of Omerta as an oath of silence has its roots in the same term, as used in Sicily, and meaning, according to Paoli's *Mafia Brotherhoods*: 'the categorical prohibition of cooperation with state authorities or reliance on its services, even when one has been victim of a crime.'

OMNIBLINK* (Degrees of Disaster) Disaster on the blinking of existence out of existence.

OMNICIEN* (Wisdom) To not only be all-knowledgable of reality but, within that construct, to also be not only the wisest entity within reality, but the wisest possible entity given the totality of all possible manifestations of entities with wisdom within reality.

OMNICLYSMIC* (Chaos and Order) A state of a reality in which its entirety is consumed of a constant, vigorous, purposeless shifting of state, perhaps even in the physical laws which govern it.

OMNICOGNISANT* (Intelligence) Not merely being aware of all things, but having the capacity to actually think about all of them at once, as well as all their infinite interrelated permutations and possibilities.

OMNIDIMENSIONAL* (Object Sizes) As big as all the dimensions.

OMNIENTROPIC* (Chaos and Order) Literally means 'all-disordering,' a whole universe or more of not only chaos, but bonus chaos-causal potential.

OMNIGAMOS* (Party Formality) Omni = all, gamos = sex. I'm not sure how the geometry of such a thing would be accomplished, but this word means 'a universe in which all things are sex.' A cosmos of limbs and genitalia engaged.

OMNIGEDDON* (Combat) War across all of reality. Some might argue that by merely existing and consuming, all lifeforms are participating in some form of this. But things seem pretty quiet to me, relatively speaking.

OMNIGENEOUS* (Comparison in Groups of Three or More) Diverse so that every possible permutation within a given set is expressed. Different from Antipotive* in that the use of opposites in the latter builds a framework of rules that can more easily quantify their arrangement. The '-geneous' suffix is borrowed from heterogeneous. I promise to give it back.

OMNILITH* (Sizes of Earth) A rock taking up, or composing, all of reality. (See Europe's 'Final Countdown.')

OMNIQUE* (Comparison in Groups of Three or More) Like establishing the difference between chaos and order, this word describes the perfect arrangement of difference as would best express true randomness and make the system the most difficult to quantify.

OMNISCIEN* (Wisdom) A level of wisdom that is best thought of as one of the résumé prerequisites for being a just god.

OMNOCALYPSE* (Degrees of Disaster) A life-extinction event, without any survivors, on a planetary scale. Notable for its comprehensive execution.

ONE-DOG NIGHT** (Temperature by Degrees) Borrowed from sled-dog slang and meaning so cold that surviving the night would require the body heat of one sled dog.

ONE-HUNDRED-DOG NIGHT** (Temperature by Degrees) Borrowed from sled-dog slang and meaning so cold that surviving the night would require the combined body heat of one-hundred sled dogs.

OORT GLACIER* (Degrees of Ice) A vast clump of ice, oortberg is to iceberg as Oort glacier is to a regular Earth glacier.

OORT SHELF* (Degrees of Ice) Oort shelf is to Oort glacier as ice shelf is to a regular Earth glacier.

OORT CAP* (Degrees of Ice) Oort cap is to Oort shelf as ice cap is to a regular ice shelf.

OORTBERG* (Degrees of Ice) A moonish-sized hunk of ice floating in space like an iceberg, perhaps as part of the Oort cloud, the source of comets, a vast field of ice surrouding much of the solar system.

OXTALITH* (Sizes of Earth) A hunk of rock the size of octillion regular boulders. That's 1,000,000,000,000,000,000,000,000,000 rocks. I propose 'oxta-' as a new metric prefix meaning 'octillion,' being the next step past the macro-limitation of 'yotta.' (See Oxtilith*.)

OXTANNUM[*] (Segments of Time) An octillion, or 1,000,000,000,00 0,000,000,000,000,000 years.

OXTAPARSEC[*] (The Distance Between Two Points) An octillion parsecs. Hardly walkable.

OXTILITH[*] (Sizes of Earth) Rock on the scale of one-octillionth of your average boulder. I have here created a new metric prefix beyond the previous micro-limitation of yocto. The 'oxti-' prefix means 'one-oxtillionth.' The 'ox' is a half-id-babble reference to the 'strength of an ox' and channels the oomph of that hand-gesture-demanding phrase into prefix boost. Also, sounds similar to the 'oct-' prefix that helps distinguish octillion's quantity.

OXTIMETER[*] (The Distance Between Two Points) One divided by an octillion meters.

OVATION[**] (Failure to Success) An ovation is a sort of quasi-triumph, the over-the-top victory parades of Roman lore. Only when compared to a proper triumph does this event appear to be any less than a huge deal.

OVERGOOGOLMETER[*] (The Distance Between Two Points) I'm introducing 'overgoogol-' as a metric prefix meaning 'unit divided by a googol' because when you do that, you put the thing over googol, to show that it's being divided. A googol is expressed as a one with a hundred zeroes behind it. Just look at it: 10,000,000,000,000,000,000,000,000,000,0 00,000,000,000,000,000,000,000,000,0000,000,000,000,000,000,000, 000,000,000,000,000,000,000,000,000. Beautiful.

OVERGOOGOLPLEXOMETER[*] (The Distance Between Two Points) I'm introducing 'overgoogolplexo-' as a metric prefix meaning 'unit divided by googolplex' because when you do that, you put the thing over googolplex, to show that it's being divided. A googolplex is expressed as a one with a google zeroes in front of it. I wanted to write it out, but as eloquently described by Carl Sagan in my favorite book of all time, *Cosmos*: 'A piece of paper large enough to have all the zeroes in googolplex written out explicitly could not be stuffed into the known universe.' Understandably, my publisher wouldn't allow it.

OWEN* (The Speed of Multipedal Locomotion) The fastest human speed, named after Jesse Owens, legendary sprinter known best for his triumph at the 1936 Summer Olympics in Berlin, Germany.

PANAMAZILE* (Bodies of Water) A river larger than any on Earth, as if all of Eurasia drained into a single basin and a single Panamazile led it out to sea.

PANBRANOPIRE* (Size of Political Entities) A nation whose jurisdiction is a brane.

PANCONTOPOLIS* (Urban Growth) A contiguous city spanning a whole continent.

PANGEIC* (Object Sizes) Size on the scale of Pangea, the supercontinent roughly the size of all our current continents lumped together.

PANGALACTOGEDDON* (Combat) Combat engulfing the whole of a galaxy. Using black holes as bullets, jockeying wormholes, GRBs as lasers, instant extinction of thousands of intelligent species, the whole nine quintillion yards.

PANGALACTOPIRE* (Size of Political Entities) A nation whose jurisdiction fills out an entire galaxy.

PANGALACTOPOLIS* (Urban Growth) A city filling out a whole galaxy. Would usually, but not necessarily, qualify as a Kardashev 2 civilization.

PANGEACLASM* (Degrees of Disaster) A super-continent scale geologic event which would, as a side effect, extinguish all life, but in its primary description, a rearrangement of the planet. As if Pangea were flipped like a pancake.

PANGEACLYSM* (Degrees of Disaster) Disaster on the scale of the complete rearrangement of continents by geologic upheaval.

PANGEDDON* (Combat) Combat resulting in the destruction of a large amount of the crust of a planet.

PANGEOCALYPSE* (Degrees of Disaster) Disaster on the scale of the destruction not just of continents, but of the better part of the crust of a planet.

PANGEOPOLIS* (Urban Growth) A city taking up an area the size of Pangea. Basically covering all exposed landmass.

PANPIRE* (Size of Political Entities) A single nation swathing across two continents. (See Archpire*)

PANPIRE A.K.A PLATEAU* (Degrees of Taxonomic Elements) Building on the Kindom and Empire words at the top of the biological catergories, using my own imperial and nation-size top-end descriptions. This whole set of words is a longshot at re-scoping academia's own taxonomy, building out from the top of the biological taxonomic pyramid. Definitely up for debate; I'd love to hear more ideas on this.

PANSOLAPIRE* (Size of Political Entities) A nation that entirely fills up the space in a solar system.

PANSOLAPOLIS⁕ (Urban Growth) A city taking up all of the space in a solar system.

PANSPERMIAL ANTICLASM, THE⁕ (Degrees of Life) That whole of life, if it exists from a contiguous source beyond earth, as proposed in the panspermia hypothesis. Basically that the earliest earthly life-forms might have been survivors of some microscopic meteor-riding source or the like, similar to how coconuts that float between islands in the Pacific spread palm trees. Anticlasm being a sort of reverse cataclysm, as I here represent that growth of life against the dead universe which exists where it isn't.

PANUNIVERPIRE⁕ (Size of Political Entities) A nation whose jurisdiction is a whole universe.

PANUNIVERPOLIS⁕ (Urban Growth) A city taking up a whole universe.

PANUNIVEGEDDON⁕ (Combat) A cosmic war consuming a whole universe.

PARAGONIC⁕ (You Did a __ Job) A paragon is a diamond over a hundred carats, and the word 'paragon' has come to mean the highest possible form within a given category. The highest possible competence within the catergory of human ability is 'paragonic.' Like how well you could do if you had a million years to think about it before every second during a given task, and you had a perfectly fit body with which to perform that task.

PARAMOUNT⁕ (Ultimate Power: Absolute Secular Authority) I imagine that if the Roman Empire had continued to grow across some larger region, perhaps fully bumping into China and India, the title Emperor would no longer have been sufficient to describe the absolute rulers. In fact, many empires might exist within such a political entity. I propose 'paramount' as that next step. King is to emperor as emperor is to paramount. Feminine: paramontrix. Emperor is to paramount as empire is to Plateau*.

PEDUOT* (Resentment to Gratitude) Hyper-innuot, marianas-deep gratitude. Like someone just saved your life.

PENTANNUM* (Segments of Time) Also known as a quadrillion, or 1,000,000,000,000,000 years.

PERSHING* (Military Units on Land) An army the size of the Allied Expeditionary Force commanded by John Pershing (see next entry). Usually a million or more men.

PERSHING* (Chain of Command) A one-word rank higher than marshal. Named after general and Pulitzer Prize-winner John 'Blackjack' Pershing, who had become so established and respected near the end of his tenure in the U.S. Army that congress authorized the president to elevate him to the rank of General of the Armies, a rank higher than the five-star General of the Army rank previously awarded to only George Washington posthumously. He had permission even to design his own insignia, but he never wore more than four stars (albeit gold ones). This homage is a nod to that humility.

PERSHING DOMUS* (Degrees of Male House Staff; Degrees of Female House Staff) Building off the 'Major Domus' prior, this follows the implied military officer hierarchy. See 'Chain of Command.'

PENTALITH* (Sizes of Earth) A hunk of earth roughly the size of a quadrillion boulders.

PICOLITH* (Degrees of the Sizes of Earth) One-trillionth the size of a regular boulder.

PLANETARY INTENT DEFENSE* (Degrees of Fortification) An apparatus designed to protect a planet from a willfull force attempting to take control of it. What we should have had ready at the beginning of *ID4*.

PLANETARY ISTHMUS* (Degrees of Fissure) The gap between two planets.

PLATEAU* (Size of Political Entities) The domain of a paramount. The raised topography implies a better way within.

PLURABRANOPIRE* (Size of Political Entities) A nation whose jurisdiction encompasses from two to a few branes.

PLURABRANOPOLIS* (Urban Growth) A city spanning from two to a few branes.

PLURACALYPSE* (Degrees of Disaster) An apocalyptic event on a plurality of worlds.

PLURAGALACTOGEDDON* (Combat) War spanning from two to a few galaxies.

PLURAGALACTOPIRE* (Size of Political Entities) A nation with a jurisdiction spanning from two to a few galaxies.

PLURAGALACTOPOLIS* (Urban Growth) A city spanning from two to a few galaxies.

PLURAGEDDON* (Combat) War on many worlds, like two technologically advanced species with dozens of planets to their claim fighting it out to mutual extinction.

PLURAGEOPIRE* (Size of Political Entities) A nation spanning two or more worlds.

PLURAGEOPOLIS* (Urban Growth) A city spanning two or more planets.

PLURASOLAPIRE* (Size of Political Entities) A nation reaching across two or more star systems.

PLURASOLAPOLIS* (Urban Growth) A city spanning two or more star systems.

PLURAUNIVEGEDDON* (Combat) War spread across two or more universes.

PROTOGENOI* (Creativity) A pre-existing word meaning 'proto-gods,' the initially manifested deities who would, in-turn, create the worlds they would rule. The 'idea' of a mountain or a tree is all that they would need to create the thing from scratch. From zero. This is higher god-level creative capacity.

PROTOGENOR* (Creativity) An entity capable of consistently manifesting original ideas in great quantity, over a long period of time. Like if Edison and Da Vinci lived together for a thousand years, then you took their ten best ideas. A protogenor-level entity would conceive ideas of that quality on a daily basis.

PULL A BRIAN* (Degrees of Disaster) To 'pull a Brian' is to lose one of the holy trinity of keys, wallet or mobile phone. My brother, Brian, does this a lot, to the patient begrudgement of his wife, Mary. Hi, Brian and Mary!

PULL A MUNSON** (Degrees of Disaster) See Munson**.

RAGNA-* (Prefix Hypebole) Ultra Collector's Triple-Platinum Extreme Edition. As extreme as the Ragnarok, the epic battle at the end of the world in Norse Mythology in which gods battle for the fate of existence.

RAGNAD✱ (Military Units on Land) An army composed of hundreds of millions of soldiers, upwards of a million. Enough to tip the scales of a battle between gods. (See Ragnoridel✱.)

RAGNAROK✱ (Combat) Combat on a planetary scale, like if both sides already had nukes at the beginning of World War II, and about ten times more combatants.

RAGNORIDEL✱ (Degrees of Fortification) Not just a clever technical apparatus like the Meteor Defense Complex or the Norad, but rather a solid, hard, continent-or-bigger-sized hyperfortress that can withstand heavy bombardment, and even play a effectual role in an actual Ragnarok, tipping the scales for or against the Gods or Frost Giants as per the needs of us humans.

RANCOMACHY✱ (Foreign Relations) Two warring parties both adamantly determined on the other's permanent extinction to the last man, woman, and child. Awful stuff.

RED SPOT KNOT✱ (Quantities of Wood) A knot of wood the size of Jupiter's Great Red Spot. Largely useless but for the rhyme.

RESERVE✱ (Degrees of House) 'Palace' is thus far the highest in the house order. To build on that, I've decided to borrow hierarchical terms describing amounts of gold, as reflects the wealth suggested by such a residence. A 'reserve' is any residence with a billion or more square feet of indoor space.

ROCKEFELLOW✱ (Personal Wealth) The richest man in all of history was worth perhaps as much as or more than 100 billion pounds in today's money. This word describes wealth at such a level.

ROCKETMOUTH✱ (Talkativeness) Motormouth is to turbinemouth as

---

turbinemouth is to rocketmouth. A rocket, as in the type that launches into space, is on average more powerful than a turbine.

RORQUALIC* (Object Sizes) Between huge and enormous. Reference to the Rorquals, that family of whales that includes the epic Blue Whale.

RUTHIAN** (Happiness to Sadness) A version of 'ruth,' which is already a word that indicates a particular degree of sadness.

SAY THE ONE THING EVERYONE'S THINKING* (Insult to Praise) Telling a person that one thing that is obvious to everyone but which doesn't concern the person, or that person doesn't realize about themselves (big ears, asymmetry, obesity, etc.). This is really messed up, and an uber-insult.

SCABLAND GENERATOR* (Degrees of Disaster by Newsworthiness; Bodies of Water) See Augscab*.

SCHWARZENEGGARIAN* (Physical Fitness) As fit as Governor Arnold Schwarzenegger was at his peak of fitness. Why is this higher than Herculean? Because I believe the fitness imagined by the ancient Greeks when picturing Hercules was, on average, lower than the fitness attained by the Governator at his peak, since no one back then would have been able to get that buff, or even be aware that such buffness could be attained. Given that he won six Mr. Olympia contests in a row and was noted in the 1987 *Guinness Book of World Records* as having a 'perfect' human form, I think this is an accurate positioning.

SHAMEFUL STUPEFACTION* (Shame to Pride) That state of shame where you almost owe it to the people in your presence to demonstrate your self-appall by silent admittance of your stupefying shock at your own shameful action.

Shrug* (Shame to Pride) That action re-applied as descriptor of its requisite emotion.

Six-dog night** (Temperature by Degrees) Borrowed from sled-dog slang and meaning so cold that surviving the night would require the combined body heat of six sled dogs.

Smithmouthed** (Talkativeness) In *The Matrix*, when Agent Smith welds Neo's mouth together, he can't talk, on account of his lack of mouthness. That's smithmouthed. Not very talkative, but trying to get through. Like when you're gagged.

Solablink* (Degrees of Disaster) Disaster on the scale of the blinking of a star out of existence.

Solacalypse* (Degrees of Disaster) Disaster on the scale of the exploding of a star, such as a supernova.

Solaclasm* (Degrees of Disaster) Disaster on the scale of the disruption of the structure of a star

Solaclysm* (Degrees of Disaster) Disaster on the scale of the breaking up of a star.

Solapire* (Size of Political Entities) A nation that takes up not only the planets and the star, but a large chunk of the empty space in a solar system

Solapire* (Degrees of Taxonomic Elements) See Panpire a.k.a. plateau*.

Solapolis* (Urban Growth) A city spanning a significant part of an entire solar system, not just covering the planets, but also a large portion of the space in between them.

Solid Oort sphere* (Degrees of Ice) A chunk of ice the size of a solar system, completely filled in, all the way out to the Oort cloud.

Sophic* (Degrees of Academic Degrees) A pre-existing word meaning 'one who teaches wisdom,' and here applied to mean one academic rank above 'eruditor.' Taken from the fictional universe of *The Great Beyond* (see Great Beyond, The*). In that context, it specifically means 'one who has earned ten eruditors and pulled them all into one arch-codex.' This is a degree that would take centuries of committed study to complete. Institutions that offer this degree should be called 'agora,' after the ancient philosophical meeting place that was the inspiration of the famous Raphael fresco 'The School of Athens.' See Eruditor* and Cognoscente*.

Soylent* (Disgusting to Delicious) Homage to the movie *Soylent Green* **[SPOILER ALERT!],** wherein the secret is revealed that a staple food of some future civilization is composed of its dead. This word basically means 'as gross as cannibalism.'

Stamper* (Failure to Success) **[SPOILER ALERT!]** Remember back in 1998 when there was a comet the size of Texas that was going to kill all life on Earth, and then a team of blue-collar deep-core oil drillers flew to the comet in a militarized space shuttle, drilled an 810 ft hole in it, dropped a nuke down the hole, and then the leader of that team saved us all by staying behind and sacrificing his own life to personally set off the nuke that broke the comet into two fragments which just barely missed the Himalayas and Andes at the last second? The man who pressed that button was Harry Stamper. Fun fact: A lot of people say he was the spitting image of Bruce Willis. I don't see it.

STARLIFE⁕ (Segments of Time) The average life of a star. In the neighborhood of 10 billion years, depending on the star.

STRATEGIC DEFENSE INITIATIVE⁕ (Degrees of Fortification) Basically a Norad*, but one that can also shoot down nuclear missiles in flight.

SUICIDAL MORTIFICATION⁕ (Shame to Pride) Shame so powerful, suicide is seriously contemplated.

SUPERAORTA⁕ (Roads by Size) A road from 321 to 640 lanes wide.

SUPERARTERY⁕ (Roads by Size) A road from 81 to 160 lanes wide.

SUPERBRANCH⁕ (Roads by Size) A road from 641 to 1280 lanes wide.

SUPERCAMPIAN⁕ (You Did a __ Job) Colleen Camp is a Hollywood producer who is a volcano of love and compliments. Lots of compliments. This word describes a competence so incredible it is beyond even Colleen Camp's ability to describe.

SUPERCOGITATIVE⁕ (Intelligence) A person of superlative capacity for the various facets of intelligence. On par with the great minds of all time, i.e. Da Vinci, Einstein, Aristotle, Shakespeare, Confucious, etc.

SUPERFREEWAY⁕ (Roads by Size) A road from 20 to 40 lanes across.

SUPERGODLY⁕ (Degrees of Normal and Strange) A strangeness beyond the comprehension of even divinity.

SUPERLAMBENT⁕ (Candlepower) Dangerously bright, causing burns and immediately blinding. Lambent is a word that refers to a degree of brightness.

SUPERNOVAGRAPHY** In the novel *Red Dwarf*, based on a British comedy of the same name, Coca Cola ignites 128 supernovae spelling out 'Coke Adds Life!' This word describes a font composed of supernovas.

SUPERREAL* (Degrees of Normal and Strange) Strange beyond what can exist. Also builds on 'surreal.' Distinct from 'impossible' in that a superreal thing might exist in a universe with different rules, but something impossible is utterly impossible in any manifestation of reality that can be accurately called real.

SUPERTRUNK* (Roads by Size) A road with between 2,561 and 5,120 lanes wide.

SUPREME DOMUS* (Degrees of Male House Staff; Degrees of Female House Staff) The supreme buttling authority in a palace of thousands of various house staffers.

SUPREME TAXONOMY* (Scale of Written Composition) Taxonomy is the study of the categorization of scientific concepts: kingdom, phylum, class, family, genus, order, species, etc. At the top of biology is the Biota, and a supreme taxonomy would be a comprehensive understanding of all science, which would contain the Biota as one of its subcategories. It is distinct from a Lapladex* in that it would be uncertain of its own completeness through all of the potentiality of creation and better describes a future-superunderstanding, which although complete in conceptual catergorization, does not yet know every detail of every point in reality and their interrelated qualities.

TECTONOMACHY* (Combat) War of an intensity and scale that significantly affects the geology of the planet.

TELLUSIAN* (Happiness to Sadness) Tellus, as the story goes, was a citizen of ancient Greece purported to be the world's happiest man.

GLOSSARY

To be tellusian is to be in a state of happiness so profound that at that moment, it is probable that you're the happiest person in the world.

TERABRANOPIRE (Size of Political Entities) A nation whose jurisdiction includes between 1,000,000,000,000 and 999,999,999,999,999 branes.

TERABRANOPOLIS (Urban Growth) A city spanning from 1,000,000,000,000 to 999,999,999,999,999 branes.

TERAGALACTOPIRE (Size of Political Entities) A nation whose jurisdiction reaches across a trillion or more galaxies, but at less than the universal scale.

TERAGALACTOPOLIS (Urban Growth) A city spanning from 1,000,000,000,000 to 999,999,999,999,999 galaxies.

TETRALITH (Sizes of Earth) A hunk of earth roughly the size of a trillion of your average boulders.

TERALOPOLIS (Urban Growth) Defined by location on list. In this case the metric prefix doesn't necessarily numerically apply, but is being drawn instead from the vein of prefix hyperbole.

TERRAPIRE (Size of Political Entities) A nation with de-facto, over-the-tipping point control of the whole world, but not having completely amalgamated every last nation. As if Vatican City and Madagascar were still holding out.

TERRAPIRE (Degrees of Taxonomic Elements) See Panpire a.k.a. plateau.

TERRESTRIAL (Object Sizes) On the scale of the size the Earth.

TERRIBLY VEXED (Shades of Anger) Homage to *Gladiator*, in which the villain Commodus at one point describes himself as such. It's a classic epic; I recommend it.

THREE-DOG NIGHT☆☆ (Temperature by Degrees) Borrowed from sled-dog slang and meaning so cold that surviving the night would require the combined body heat of three sled dogs.

TO GET MUNSONED☆☆ (Degrees of Disaster) See Munson☆☆.

TOPSY☆ (Chaos and Order) Well ordered and functioning. Professionally organized and goodly efficient.

TREMENDOPOLIS☆ (Urban Growth) Defined by location on list.

TRUNK☆ (Roads by Size) A road between 1,281 and 2,560 lanes wide.

TUCKERISHESQULENTNESS☆ (Talkativeness) This word refers to a talkativeness as talkative as Chris Tucker's character in *Rush Hour*. The length of this word is appropriate to the prolific verbosity of that character, and Tucker's ability to machine gun out those lines.

TURBINEMOUTH☆ (Talkativeness) Motor is to turbine as motormouth is to turbinemouth. A turbine is on average faster and more powerful than a motor.

TURVY☆ (Chaos and Order) Pure turvy, undiluted by the topsy.

TWO-DOG NIGHT☆☆ (Temperature by Degrees) Borrowed from sled-dog slang and meaning so cold that surviving the night would require the combined body heat of two sled dogs.

ULTRA-PLINIAN☆ (Shades of Anger) The biggest kind of volcano applied to describe an epic level of uber-anger. Over-the-top unbelievable, almost-comical-to-a-third-party anger. Ultra-plinian is, sort of like in hurricane and tornado scales, the highest rank on the Volcanic Explosivity Index. Definitively cataclysmic. An eruption such as that of the Toba volcano, which almost killed off the human species about 73,000 years ago. The upper end of ultra-plinian, the ultra-plinian mega colossal eruption can send upwards of a thousand cubic kilometers or more of rock into the atmosphere. Pliny the Elder described the eruption of Vesuvius and is homaged by geologists in their naming of this type of volcano after him.

UNBALLPARKABLE (Non-Numerical Elastic Quantities) So many you can't even give a ballpark estimate.

UNIVERPIRE (Size of Political Entities) A nation whose jurisdiction includes a large chunk of the universe.

UNIVERPOLIS (Urban Growth) A city taking up a large chunk of a universe.

UNIVERSAL SAVANT (Intelligence) A person with savant-like ability, but in all areas of mental capacity.

UNIVERSOLITH (Sizes of Earth) A rock that takes up, or unto itself is, a whole universe.

UNIVEGEDDON (Combat) War across a large chunk of the universe. If there were one going on by entities advanced enough to hide from each other, right this very second, how would we even know?

UTTOL (Contractual Agreements) Distinct from a Divinant* in that the powers of the gods of a divinant have limitations. An uttol is a reality-preserving agreement among parts of an omnipotent whole, such as might exist in agreement among the Holy Trinity, or Vishnu, Shiva, and the Brahman.

VAULT* (Degrees of House) 'Palace' is thus far the highest in the house order. To build on that, I've decided to borrow hierarchical terms describing amounts of gold, as reflects the wealth suggested by such a residence. A 'vault' is any residence between 500,000,000 and 999,999,999 square feet.

VON NEUMANN OMNICLASM* (Degrees of Disaster by Newsworthiness) John von Neumann was a polymath who, besides a bookshelf of scientific contribution, also described a self-replicating machine in a thought experiment in 1948. A space-worthy, nano-scale 'Grey Goo' version of this 'clanking replicator,' if let loose on the universe, could eventually consume the cosmos and reduce stars and species alike to a cosmos of nigh uncountable repetitions of the original design. Such an event would be a Von Neumann Omniclasm. Please don't build one.

WAMPOKLAK* (Resentment to Gratitude) Ultra-innuot. Id-babble term describing not how appreciative you'd be if someone just saved your life, but if someone saves the life of all your children and grandchildren. The upper limit of the human capacity for this emotional scale.

WANNUOT* (Resentment to Gratitude) Super-innuot. Derives from pure id-babble.

WILDERESQUE* (Coolness) Homage to the title character of *National Lampoon's Van Wilder*, who is, indeed, very cool.

WINNER, THE* (Darwinian Prowess) Within a given evolutionary system, a species which is so successful that the fate of all other species is a function of the winner's will. With 3.8 billion years of species clawing for continued existence, we're almost the first species to EVER get there. Go team!

YOTTALITH* (Sizes of Earth) A hunk of earth roughly the size of a septillion of your average boulders.

YOTTANNUM* (Segments of Time) One septillion, or 1,000,000,00 0,000,000,000,000,000 years.

ZAZIC* (Funniness) Reference to the ZAZ (Zucker, Abrahams, Zucker) comedy team. *Entertainment Magazine* crowned their opus *Airplane!* the funniest movie ever. Also, the feel of the word nicely matches its definition. Additionally, it conveniently builds on 'zany,' a lower form of humor. It's less than Besic* only because Besic* is a hypothetical humor that, because it references a god, describes a funny that is beyond human capacity.

ZENOMETER* (The Distance Between Two Points) See Inifinitesim-eter*.

ZETTALITH* (Sizes of Earth) A hunk of earth the size of roughly a sextillion of your average boulders.

ZETTANNUM* (Segments of Time) One sextillion, or 1,000,000,000 ,000,000,000,000 years.

ZIZIC* (Object Sizes) As big as I imagine the mythical bird Ziz to be, a prerequisite of its size being the ability to block out the sun – so acres, if not miles across.

ZIZTAG* (Military Units in the Air) Named after Ziz, the bird of the Leviathan, Ziz, and Behemoth trio. Applying '-tag' as a suffix describing forces on this scale. Ziztag is to aircraft as Behemotag* is to soldiers. See Behemotag*.